Let Them Play By All Means

Let Them Play By All Means

The story of Yorkshire Rugby Union in World War Two

STUART SHEARD

Published by Drop Kick Books
www.dropkickbooks.co.uk

ISBN 978-0-9567444-1-8

British Library Cataloguing in Publications Data

A catalogue record for this book is available from the British Library

Book and cover design by Clare Brayshaw
Team photos on cover Huddersfield Old Boys 1943/44 & Baildon 1939/40

Prepared and printed by:

York Publishing Services Ltd

64 Hallfield Road

Layerthorpe

York YO31 7ZQ

Tel: 01904 431213

Website: www.yps-publishing.co.uk

I would like to thank my wife Mary
for her support, encouragement and guidance.

Contents

Acknowledgements

Tony Collins

Bob Bowman

Richard Lowther

Tim Auty

Philip Dearnaly

Keith Barber and Judith Germaine – Leeds Corinthians RUFC

Phil Gilbank – Pocklington RUFC

Graham Reid – Baildon RUFC

Peter Thompson –Otley RUFC

Don Butler – York RUFC

Ian Johnson – Cleckheaton RUFC

Pete Fairless – Skipton RUFC

Barrie Starbuck – Huddersfield RURC

Brian Forshaw – Harrogate RUFC

Dave Butler – Old Rishworthians RUFC

Jerry Waller – Old Thornensians RUFC

Mike Bidgood – Leeds Carnegie RUFC

Phil Fowler – York Railway Institute RUFC

Adrian Hartman – Selby RUFC

Harry Edgar – Rugby League Journal

The Rugby League Archives – The University of Huddersfield

Michael Rowe – The Rugby Football Union

Richard Byram and Jayne Marsden – The Yorkshire Post

Joanne Stephens and Ian Leask – Yorkshire RFU

I would like to thank the Yorkshire Post, the Hull Daily Mail and the Craven Herald for giving me permission to use a number of the photographs and illustrations in this book.

Introduction

Why did some rugby union clubs in Yorkshire continue to play through one of the most difficult periods in the history of this country?

This is my story of what happened to Yorkshire Rugby Union during the Second World War. The title is taken from a quote by Mr R.F. (Bob) Oakes, the Honorary Secretary of the Yorkshire Rugby Football Union. You will find the whole quote in Chapter Two. It is a story that begins in the 1930s and ends in 1946. The Chapters that follow will describe how the Yorkshire Rugby Football Union and its clubs reacted to the declaration of war on 3rd September 1939. Some of the clubs continued to play regular fixtures right through wartime while others ceased activities immediately war was declared. There was also a group of clubs that played through the first year or two and then closed down and remarkably one or two clubs that only played during wartime, ceasing activities when the war ended. I hope to be able to highlight some of the factors that affected the Yorkshire clubs and how they responded to those factors. It has been difficult to find many people who can give first hand contemporary accounts of wartime rugby, and so to a large extent this story is my interpretation of the recorded events of the time. Many were quite unusual and unexpected. There were many challenges to overcome so that young men would have the opportunity to take part in sport, a very necessary distraction, at a most difficult time. Morale is a very important factor in any struggle for survival and I am sure that the opportunity to play or watch a game of rugby must have boosted the morale of the people involved.

Later in this story I will consider the role of the National Governing Body, the Rugby Football Union (RFU), and how the RFU, based in

London, reacted to the World War. I will also examine the way in which the relationship between rugby union and rugby league was affected at both local and National level, and how both codes responded. Services teams had a considerable impact on rugby, both locally and nationally. This was another important factor to consider when telling the story of wartime rugby union in Yorkshire.

Many dramatic and life changing events took place in Britain and across the World between 1939 and 1945. How those events impacted on the sport at all levels will be an important background to this story. I hope that what follows will paint a picture of a sport struggling to survive against a backdrop of World War.

Chapter One

The 1930s

By the beginning of the 1930s, rugby union in Yorkshire was beginning to recover from the loss in 1895 of some its strongest clubs following the dispute over broken time payments that led to the formation of the Northern Union. The number of clubs in Yorkshire seemed to have stabilised during the 1930s. There were one hundred and six clubs in membership of the Yorkshire Rugby Football Union in the 1930/31 season, a figure that had increased to one hundred and eight by the beginning of the 1938/39 season.

However, despite this apparent stability, concerns were raised at the 1939 Yorkshire Annual Meeting regarding a decline in individual County membership from four hundred and eighty three members in 1933/34 to three hundred and forty seven members in 1938/39.

Rugby Union

NORTHERN CLUB RECORDS

FINAL TABLE

	P.	W.	D	L.	For	Agst.
Barnsley	25	12	3	10	198	210
Batley	30	8	5	17	213	376
Birkenhead Pak	27	15	10	2	318	220
Blaydon	25	7	3	15	115	207
Bradford	31	19	0	12	517	344
Bramley O.B.	28	18	4	6	324	180
Brighouse Rangers	30	21	4	5	411	115
Broughton Park	28	9	1	18	200	361
Carlisle	24	17	2	5	295	108
Castleford	26	22	2	2	338	91
Cockermouth	32	28	2	2	527	86
Darlington	29	13	3	13	203	210
Durham City	32	22	2	8	324	180
Furness	21	12	1	8	297	124
Fylde	31	13	3	15	272	265
Gateshead Fell	25	10	5	10	169	178
Gosforth	23	10	0	13	199	266
Halifax	31	14	4	13	304	313
Harrogate O.B.	33	12	2	19	282	326
Hartlepool O.B.	25	13	4	8	195	151
Hartlepool Rovers	31	17	5	9	332	223
Headingley	28	21	2	5	345	205
Heaton Moor	31	3	5	23	163	406
Hessle	25	17	2	6	396	144
Huddersfield O.B.	32	18	5	9	300	222
Hull	27	15	1	11	388	210
Ilkley	32	10	2	20	212	338
Kendal	34	29	0	5	462	133
Leeds Univ	31	13	1	17	282	230
Liverpool	25	8	1	16	180	274
Liverpool Univ.	31	18	2	11	343	263
Manchester	29	20	2	7	495	258
Manchester Univ.	31	12	3	16	245	299
Middlesbrough	26	16	3	7	283	148
Morley	32	24	3	5	443	184
New Brighton	27	19	0	8	331	160
North Durham	26	11	3	12	252	218
Northern	25	17	1	7	360	173
Old Leodiensians	30	19	2	9	374	222
Old Novos	23	8	1	14	187	236
Old Roundhegians	26	18	2	6	318	151
Otley	32	19	1	12	305	279
Percy Park	29	22	5	2	389	143
Port Sunlight	27	14	0	13	271	204
Preston Grasshoppers	23	8	4	11	166	223
Rockcliffe	28	4	2	22	160	383
Rotherham	23	13	2	8	233	153
Ryton	22	5	3	14	88	153
Roundhay	33	11	1	21	231	429
Sale	31	21	2	8	317	180
Scarborough	33	22	6	5	383	201
St. Helens	31	19	0	12	381	262
Skipton	30	14	1	15	246	307
Sunderland	24	10	4	10	130	121
Tyldesley	25	15	4	6	254	150
Tynedale	27	11	3	13	258	229
Wakefield	35	19	2	14	291	268
Waterloo	32	19	2	11	383	210
Vatoe	27	19	2	6	398	156
West Hartlepool	28	14	2	12	271	255
Wigan O.B.	27	14	2	11	242	193
Wilmslow	27	20	2	5	470	159
Winnington Park	29	17	1	11	267	188

Club Records 1938-39

The main reason for the concerns appears to be that, because of the decline in membership and the subsequent loss of income from the member subscriptions, the County had made a loss on its activities in the 1938/39 season. The concerns of members and clubs, raised at the Annual Meeting, were dismissed by the Honorary Secretary, Bob Oakes, who said at the County meeting that there was nothing wrong with Yorkshire Rugby Union and decried '*vapourings in the press which spoke of revolutionary movements. All over the United Kingdom clubs on all games- excepting the top notchers- were grousing about their receipts.*' Mr Oakes praised the enthusiasm amongst the junior clubs, which he said was most heartening. He also urged club officials to submit their fixtures for inclusion in the 1939/40 handbook immediately. He informed County members that there were still thirty clubs that had not submitted their 1939/40 fixture lists.

Mr R.F. Oakes

Did the clubs that had not submitted fixtures have access to some type of crystal ball? Did they know for certain that war was imminent and that there was little point in submitting a list of fixtures that would never be played? I doubt that was the case. It was probably more to do with changes of secretary during the close season and ongoing discussions with potential opponents regarding fixture dates. However, the majority of people who attended that Yorkshire meeting in the Metropole Hotel, in Leeds, on 26th June 1939, will have been very aware of the newspaper headlines and the radio broadcasts that had been forecasting war for a number of years. Life in Britain was changing and all the indicators at the time seemed to point to further changes and possibly a war that would dramatically affect the way of life for everyone.

However, despite all that was happening in the world, it appears from contemporary reports that nobody present at the 1939 Yorkshire Rugby Football Union Annual Meeting raised any concerns regarding the future of Yorkshire rugby in the event of war being declared. Were they hoping for the best or simply ignoring what was happening in the world outside Yorkshire rugby? We must assume that there must have been people involved with Yorkshire rugby who thought that contingency plans should have been discussed. However, it appeared that no official discussions or announcements regarding the possible impact of war on rugby union were made at the Annual Meeting. In his annual message to the County printed in the 1939/40 Yorkshire handbook, the Past President of the RFU, Mr W.T. Pearce, began with the following quotation by Edmund Burke, *'No men can act with effect who do not act in concert; no men can act in concert who do not act in confidence; no men can act with confidence who are not bound together by common opinions, common affections and common interests.'* Mr Pearce then said the following in his explanation about why he thought the quote was relevant to the game of rugby, *'These words were meant to apply to matters of much greater importance, and yet they deserve attention by anyone engaging in teamwork, whether in the form of business responsibilities or sport. Do they not apply with equal appositeness to the international position, in which anyone worth his salt is personally involved in one way or another? At the time of writing this, the 'peace' has not been broken, and one may be pardoned for being optimistic enough to hope that in spite of the ugly words being spoken and printed about one another, the contending parties may come to the conference table at no far distant date without plunging into War.'*

Mr W.T. Pearce

Mr Pearce continued the optimistic tone of his message with his hope that war would not break out. The rest of the message is concerned with discussing the importance of rugby being based on *'common opinions, common affections and common interests.'* The fact that Mr Pearce's message to the County was written on 5th August 1939 must indicate that he was a genuine optimist who, despite all that was happening, still believed that war could be avoided and that rugby would continue as before.

In the world away from rugby the reality was very different. The preparations for war across Europe have been thoroughly documented many times. My intention here is to give a picture of a reality that contrasts sharply with the optimism of some rugby men in 1939. In 1935 the production of gas masks began and following an Act of Parliament in 1937 those gas masks were delivered to local stores ready for distribution. The same Act of Parliament saw the beginning of the construction of air raid shelters. These were, of course, not the only signs that war was likely; evacuation and rationing plans had been drawn up during the 1930s. Air raid wardens had been appointed and trained and while all these plans were made and implemented the headlines in the newspapers, both local and national, must have left people in little doubt about the likely hood of war. As we moved nearer to 1939, Adolph Hitler had begun to take aggressive action against Germany's immediate neighbours and was making warlike announcements that seemed to provide even more evidence that Germany had every intention of invading those neighbours and so provoking a war with Britain. On 12th August 1938, German troops were mobilised and an invasion of Czechoslovakia looked very likely. It was these provocative actions that prompted the British Prime Minister, Neville Chamberlain, to travel to Munich to discuss the deteriorating situation with the German Chancellor Adolph Hitler. The infamous 'Peace in our time' agreement reached in Munich, and signed by the British Prime Minister Neville Chamberlain and Adolph Hitler, was the outcome of those talks. Perhaps the piece of paper that Chamberlain waved to the waiting media when he arrived back in Britain gave some people hope that war had been averted. Those hopes were dashed of course, when, despite the agreement that said they would not invade Czechoslovakia, German troops entered that country on 3rd March 1939.

Against this background, the Yorkshire Rugby Football Union, in June 1939, still appeared to assume that there would not be a war and that the 1939/40 season would take place as normal. The national picture was no different. The Rugby Football Union's responses to what was happening in the world were very similar to those in Yorkshire. At the RFU Annual Meeting in June 1939, the discussions that were reported mainly concerned rule changes, the resumption of international fixtures against France and preparations for an Australian touring team due to arrive in England in September 1939. If contingency plans in the event of war were discussed, they did not receive any press coverage and the prevailing mood seemed to be to carry on as normal and hope for the best.

I recognise that it may have been very difficult for officials at the Rugby Football Union and the Yorkshire RFU to plan for an event they hoped would not happen. Perhaps discussions did take place and a decision was made that those responsible for administering rugby union should wait and see and react accordingly. After all, rugby union was an amateur sport and apart from a few full-time employees at Twickenham and perhaps the grounds man, cleaners and bar staff at some of the senior clubs, few people's lively hood was threatened if rugby union did not continue to be played during wartime. Conscription which began in April 1939 had not really affected the clubs as the 1938/39 season had ended before conscription began. So it was perhaps understandable that rugby people were apparently looking forward optimistically to the 1939/40 season with similar hopes for peace to those of Mr W.T. Pearce.

In Yorkshire, the 21st October 1939 had been agreed as the date for the annual County fixture against Ulster in Belfast, with Yorkshire's first County Championship match against Cumberland scheduled for 4th November. The County Championship was a very important part of the rugby scene in Yorkshire. 1927/28 had been the last season that Yorkshire had been the dominant county in the country. In fact in 1938/39 they were not even the strongest county in the North. In the Northern Division of the County Championship in 1938/39 Cheshire had won this accolade, a position Yorkshire would hope to challenge in 1939/40.

For many of the clubs Saturday 9th September 1939 would be the date when the first fixtures of the season were expected to be played. Not all clubs started on the first Saturday of the season, some clubs having practice matches planned for the 9th September with their official start to the season being a week or two later. There were some interesting fixtures planned for that second Saturday in September. Headingley had a fixture away at Bedford while Yorkshire Cup winners Morley had arranged an away fixture at Halifax. Leeds Chirons, the club I played for in the 1960s, had a practice match planned for the 9th September and were expecting to begin their season on 16th September away to Halifax Collegians. Ironically, Old Roundhegians did not think that Chirons were playing a practice match on 9th September. According to the Old Roundhegians fixture list, Chirons were due to play them on the 9th September, Old Roundhegians making the short walk from Roundhay School to Soldiers Field for the away fixture. It also appeared that on the 16th September Chirons were similarly double booked as, according to the West

LEEDS CHIRONS

	1st Team		2nd Team	
Date	*Opponents*	*At*	*Opponents*	*At*
Sep. 9	Practice	h	Practice	h
16	Halifax Collegians	a	Halifax Collegians 'A'	h
23	Yarnbury	h	Yarnbury 'A'	a
30	West Leeds Old Boys	a	West Leeds O.B. 'A'	h
Oct. 7	Leeds Training College	h	LeedsTraining Coll. 'A'	a
14	Castleford	h	Castleford 'A'	a
21	Heath Old Boys	a	Heath Old Boys 'A'	h
28	Bohemians	h	Bohemians 'A'	a
Nov. 4	Leeds Y.M.C.A.	h	Leeds Y.M.C.A. 'A'	a
11	Burley	a	Burley 'A'	h
18	Bingley	a	Bingley 'A'	h
25	Moortown	h	Moortown 'A'	a
Dec. 2	Leeds Training College	a	Leeds Training Coll.'A'	h
9	Heath Old Boys	h	Heath Old Boys 'A'	a
16	Bohemians	a	Bohemians 'A'	h
23				
Jan. 6	Headingley Old Boys	a	Headingley O.B. 'A'	h
13	Yarnbury	a	Yarnbury 'A'	h
20	Leeds Salem	a	Leeds Salem 'A'	h
27	Headingley Old Boys	h	Headingley O.B. 'A'	a
Feb. 3	Bingley	h	Bingley 'A'	a
10	Leeds Y.M.C.A.	a	Leeds Y.M.C.A. 'A'	h
17	West Leeds Old Boys	h	West Leeds O.B. 'A'	a
24	Moortown	a	Moortown 'A'	h
Mar. 2	Burley	h	Burley 'A'	a
9	Carnegie	a		
16	Leeds Salem	h	Leeds Salem 'A'	a
23	Carnegie	h		
30	Castleford	a	Castleford 'A'	h
Apr. 6	Halifax Collegians	h	Halifax Collegians 'A'	a

Hon. Sec.—W. I. Davies, 22 Rossall Road, Leeds 8.
Hon. Team Sec.—G. H. Pollard, 6 Glossop View, Leeds 6.
Hon. Treas.—G. M. Dorney, 1 Hollin Drive, Leeds 6.
Captains—A. Rouse. 2nd Team, T. Jaffe.
Ground—Roundhay car from Briggate to Oakwood. Turn left up Old Park Road.
Dressing Rooms—Roundhay School, Old Park Road, Oakwood.
Headquarters—Oak Hotel, Headingley, Leeds.
Day and Time of Weekly Meeting—
Club Colours—Black and white jerseys; black shorts.
Result of Matches 1938-39—Played 23, won 10, lost 10, drawn 3. Points for, 193; against, 239.

223

Leeds Chirons 1939-40 Fixtures – The season that did not happen

Leeds High School Old Boys fixture list, they were due to play a home fixture against Chirons.

How those fixture problems were resolved will, I hope, become clear in chapter two. However, it was not fixture clashes that people believed would be the main pre-occupations of the Yorkshire clubs and officials in the 1939/40 season. It was expected to be the impact of some of the rule changes agreed at the RFU Annual Meeting, the increasing concerns about the declining County membership and the problems of rugby union expansion.

We have to assume that, despite all indicators pointing to war, the Yorkshire clubs will have begun pre-season training during the summer of 1939, possibly reflecting some of the optimism of W.T. Pearce. However, as it got closer to the beginning of the season, many of the players who would have been working on their fitness on those warm summer evenings must have thought that perhaps all the training would be in vain and no rugby would be played in September 1939. Even so, as August wound to a close, the newspaper headlines and editorials in the Yorkshire Post still had a hint of optimism. On the 26th August 1939 the Yorkshire Post editorial had the headline '*Grave Situation*', but the article still held out some hope that the last minute peace talks involving Germany and the British Ambassador would be successful. However, by the 29th August it seemed clear from the Yorkshire Post that, despite the apparent optimism of the editorial on the 26th August, the talks were in fact doomed to failure. All the signs were that war was imminent. Preparations continued across the country, so that on 1st September, the Yorkshire Post was able to announce that Britain was '*A Nation Prepared*'.

On the 1st September Germany invaded Poland and, because of the treaty that Britain had signed with Poland, war was now inevitable. Some of the senior clubs such as Bradford, Headingley and Hull and East Riding had practice matches planned for Saturday 2nd September. I think it is quite possible that those practice matches did take place as it wasn't clear, even at that late stage, when the declaration of war would come. Baildon also organised a sevens but as there were only three teams taking part, Baildon, Baildon 'A' and Bingley, it was decided to play eleven a side games. Baildon won the event. It appears from contemporary newspaper reports to be one of the few games Bingley played in the 1939/40 season.

The evacuation of children from areas likely to be bombed had begun on 1st September and over 90,000 children were expected to leave Leeds over the next few days. Soccer and rugby league matches were scheduled for Saturday the 2nd of September and those fixtures took place. John Wilson, the Secretary of the Rugby Football League, said that all fixtures would be fulfilled until the government either ordered or requested that play should cease. The Football Association also made an announcement that actually quoted advice from the Home Office which said that the current situation did not warrant the cancellation of matches. It was the second Saturday of the new season and both sports obviously thought it important not to disrupt the start to the season by reacting prematurely. Cricket, on the other hand, did react and although local league matches continued, the County Championship games were cancelled.

1st Team **BAILDON** **2nd Team**

Date	*Opponents* (1st Team)	*At*		*Opponents* (2nd Team)	*At*	
Sep. 9	Bradford Salem	a	...	Bradford Salem 'A'	h	...
16	Scarborough	h	...			
23	Wetherby	a	...	Wetherby 'A'	h	...
30	Upper Wharfedale	h	...			
Oct. 7	Sandal	a	...	Sandal 'A'	h	...
14	Bingley	h	...	Bingley 'A'	a	...
21	York	a	...	York 'A'	h	...
28	Upper Wharfedale	a	...	Bradford 'B'	h	...
Nov. 4	Castleford	a	...	Castleford 'A'	h	...
11	Huddersfield Y.M.C.A.	h	...	Huddsfd. Y.M.C.A. 'A'	a	...
18	Brighouse Rangers	a	...	Brighouse Rangers 'A'	h	...
25	Bradford Salem	h	...	Bradford Salem 'A'	a	...
Dec. 2	Nab Wood	a	...	Nab Wood 'A'	h	...
9	Wibsey	h	...	Wibsey 'A'	a	...
16	Leeds Y.M.C.A.	a	...	Leeds Y.M.C.A. 'A'	h	...
23	Keighlians	h	...	Keighlians 'A'	a	...
30	Wibsey	a	...	Wibsey 'A'	h	...
Jan. 6	Nab Wood	h	...	Nab Wood 'A'	a	...
13	Ossett	a	...	Ossett 'A'	h	...
20	Bradford Extra 1st.	a	...			
27	Bingley	a	...	Bingley 'A'	h	...
Feb. 3	Brighouse Rangers	h	...	Brighouse Rangers 'A'	a	...
10	Keighlians	a	...	Keighlians 'A'	h	...
17	York	h	...	York 'A'	a	...
24	Otley 'A'	a	...	Otley 'B'	h	...
Mar. 2	Ossett	h	...	Ossett 'A'	a	...
9	Huddersfield Y.M.C.A.	a	...	Huddsfd. Y.M.C.A. 'A'	h	...
16	Castleford	h	...	Castleford 'A'	a	...
23	Otley 'A'	h	...	Otley 'B'	a	...
30	Wetherby	h	...	Wetherby 'A'	a	...
Apr. 6	Scarborough	a	...			
13	Sandal	h	...	Sandal 'A'	a	...
20	Bradford Extra 1st.	h	...	Bradford 'B'	a	...

Hon. Sec.—J. S. ARMSTRONG, 33 Ferncliffe Drive, Baildon (*Tel.* Office, Bradford 8154). *Hon. Fixture Sec.*—J. W. FRASER, Cecil Avenue, Baildon (*Tel.* Shipley 464). *Hon. Treas.*—J. MARRINER, Fairmount, Parkside, Bingley (*Tel.* Home, Bingley 758).
Captain—F. LEEMING.
Ground—Blythwick, Baildon Bridge. Five minutes' from Shipley Station on the Otley Road; just over the bridge.
Dressing Rooms—On ground.
Headquarters—Angel Hotel, Baildon (*Tel.* Shipley 1415).
Day and Time of Weekly Meeting—Monday, 8.0. p.m.
Club Colours—Red, black, and white.
Result of Matches 1938-39—Played 28, won 16, lost 9, drawn 3. Points for, 323; against, 244.

163

Baildon's plans for 1939-40

The 2nd September was, in effect, the last day of the 1939/40 season for both soccer and rugby league. It is very difficult to imagine the feelings of the players and spectators at those fixtures. Were they making the most of the last Saturday of 'normality'? Or did some of the people involved still cling to the hope that a last minute solution would be found and the 9th September would see another full fixture list? The reality of the situation became clear when at 11.00am on Sunday 3rd September Prime Minister Neville Chamberlain made his radio broadcast announcing that Britain had declared war on Germany. The announcement was hardly unexpected but it did signal the beginning of a period when life in Britain would change drastically. Many people believed that this war would have much more impact on the majority of ordinary people and their everyday lives than had the Great War. Weapons were much more sophisticated and aircraft and ships had improved out of all recognition. The preparations that took place in Britain during the 1930s seemed to support the view that a second World War would be a different type of conflict to the one fought between 1914 and 1918. Germany would be targeting British cities and towns and ordinary citizens as well as fighting our troops in Europe.

How would British sport and in particular rugby union react?

Chapter Two

The Declaration of War

The declaration of war, when it came at 11.00 am on Sunday 3rd September, was of course hardly unexpected. The preparations for war had accelerated over the previous two or three weeks but not, it seemed, on the sporting front. Unlike soccer and rugby league, sports that traditionally began their season in late August, the rugby union season hadn't yet begun. I imagine that the sportsmen who sat and listened to the broadcast by Neville Chamberlain, in which he announced the beginning of World War Two, may well have thought that there would no further action on the sporting field for the foreseeable future. The expectations were that the hostilities would begin immediately and that most young men involved in amateur sport would either be called up to the forces or would be working long hours in reserved occupations, helping the war effort. Sport, and games of rugby in particular, probably did not seem at all likely to be taking place given the grave situation that Britain was now facing.

The Yorkshire Rugby Football Union's reaction, at an emergency meeting held at the Metropole Hotel in Leeds on Monday 4th September, seemed to confirm every rugby union player's worst fears about the future. *'All fixtures were to be cancelled until further notice and no additional fixtures should be arranged.'* This ruling was to apply to every club in membership. The gloomy scenario painted by the Yorkshire RFU announcement meant that many young men will have assumed that their rugby playing days were over. What was going to happen in the future would be very much dependant on how the war progressed and thoughts of playing sport must be dismissed from their minds as the future of their country and way of life was at stake.

The Saturday that followed the declaration of war must really have confirmed every sportsman's worst fears. Very little sport was played in Yorkshire on Saturday 9th September 1939. One rugby union game took place at Huddersfield Old Boys Ground at Waterloo. A team from the Artillery played a team from the Infantry and a number of Huddersfield players took part in this game. The only other rugby game played that Saturday was a hastily arranged rugby league match played at Crown Flatt Dewsbury Rugby League Club's ground. This game was played for the benefit of the New Zealand tourists who were, because of the declaration of war, having to return home the following week before their tour had really begun. New Zealand won the game in front of a crowd of over 6,000. The gate receipts of £487 were given to the tourists to assist with some of their expenses. However, despite the lack of organised sport on 9th September 1939, both the soccer and rugby league authorities were discussing the setting up of a wartime competition. It was widely expected that both sports would recommence fairly quickly. What was going to happen in rugby union?

It appeared from all the newspaper reports that the sport of rugby union, certainly at club level, was not going to take place during World War Two. At an RFU meeting on 12th September that, because of the travel restrictions, only the London based members of the committee attended made the following resolutions:

a) All fixtures already arranged be cancelled

b) A moratorium on all outstanding loans be declared

c) All subscriptions and season ticket payments made in advance be repaid

d) The Honorary Treasurer and Honorary Secretary were authorised to incur minimum expenditure to maintain Twickenham

The situation seemed very clear from both the RFU and Yorkshire announcements. Rugby union was not going to be played during the Second World War. The country was focussing on the war effort and the sport should not be played until the war was won. However, despite all the official announcements to the contrary, club rugby union in Yorkshire resumed. The Yorkshire RFU had decided to distribute the 1939/40 handbook despite the fact that they had announced that none of the fixtures contained in the handbook should take place. Perhaps it was assumed that as the handbook had been printed, it should be sent to clubs and County members in the hope that the war would soon be over, clubs could resume their activities, and may even be able to play some of the fixtures they had organised for 1939/40 later in the season. That did not prove to be the case and the 1939/40 handbook is now a unique record of what might have been. Many clubs did gradually re-start activities but what took place was very different to that envisioned when the Yorkshire handbook went to print in August 1939.

Bob Oakes, the Yorkshire Secretary, made an announcement that seemed to encourage the resumption of activities when he said, '*At the moment there is little than can be done officially, but if thirty people can find a football and a field then let them play by all means.*' This statement appeared in the Yorkshire Post on 13th September 1939 and was supported by comments made by the rugby union representative J.M. Kilburn who said, '*It should not be thought that the playing of rugby union football is forbidden or would meet with official disapproval. Clubs in evacuated areas are not allowed to open their grounds to the public but in areas where public entertainment is permitted rugby union football can take place along with every other organised sport.*' On Saturday 16th September club games re-started. The response to Mr Oakes announcement seems to have been fairly rapid. The reality was that although fixtures appeared to have been ruled out by the Yorkshire RFU many clubs still had players and officials and arranging a fixture at short notice would not have proved too difficult. The fixtures that were arranged were not, of course, those listed in the 1939/40 handbook. Most of the games that did take place initially were local derbies. These games arranged at very short notice had to take account of the travel restrictions and the petrol rationing that came into force on the 16th September. Ironically, following the announcement from the Yorkshire Secretary, Bob Oakes, the RFU reversed their position and announced that after another meeting of the London members, clubs would now be allowed to carry on playing if they were able and wished to do so.

For one club the outbreak of war could not have come at a worst time. Old Thornensians, old boys of Thorne Grammar School, were formed in 1939 and had planned a full fixture list for the 1939/40 season beginning on 23rd September with a home fixture against a Hessle XV. As those fixtures had been cancelled and the majority of their players had been called up, the club had to put its plans on hold before it could even start playing. A few school versus old boys fixtures were played on an 'ad hoc' basis but it would be 1946 before the club could begin playing fixtures.

OLD THORNENSIANS

1st Team

Date	*Opponents*	*At*	*Opponents*	*At*
Sep. 9	Practice	h		
16	Practice	h		
23	Hessle 'A'	h		
30				
Oct. 7	Old Wathonians	h		
14				
21	Hessle 'A'	a		
28				
Nov. 4	Wakefield 'A'	a		
11	Old Wathonians	a		
18	Sheffield 'B'	h		
25	Vickers Steel	a		
Dec. 2	Old Hilmians	a		
9				
16	Barnsley 'A'	a		
23				
30	Sheffield Tigers 'A'	h		
Jan. 6				
13				
20	Selby 'A'	h		
27	Sheffield 'B'	a		
Feb. 3				
10	Old Hilmians	h		
17				
24				
Mar. 2				
9	Vickers Steel	h		
16	Hull University	a		
23	Rotherham 'A'	a		
30	Selby 'A'	a		
Apr. 6	Rotherham 'A'	h		
13	Barnsley 'A'	h		

Hon. Sec. and Treas.—WALTER W. JONES-LEE, Grammar School, Thorne, Doncaster (*Tel.* Thorne 2179).

Captain—

Ground—2 miles form North or South Railway Stations. 5 minutes from Goole and Doncaster bus routes. (Grammar School).

Dressing Rooms—At the School.

Headquarters—At the School.

Day and Time of Weekly Meeting—Monday at 7.30 p.m.

Club Colours—Royal blue, black and white hoops.

258

The fixtures Old Thornensians had planned for the 1939-40 season

I imagine that whatever had been said officially by the RFU and Yorkshire some clubs would probably have attempted to arrange fixtures. Many of the young men called up were still in Britain training and preparing for active service.

In early September conscription was having an impact on some clubs but there were others that had not been as badly affected. Many of the young men that had been called up were training in their local area and so would be returning home on leave. Often that leave coincided with an opportunity to return to their club for a game of rugby. So the 1939/40 season began and although it did not resemble the one that had been planned, after a stuttering start games began to take place on a regular basis.

One of the first fixtures to take place was in Halifax. This was a local derby between Halifax and Old Rishworthians played at Ovenden Park, Halifax's home ground. In fact, as the Yorkshire Post's J.M. Kilburn commented in an article in the newspaper on 20th September, '*Halifax District shows the way.'* He then went on to make the following comments on the current situation, *'Rugby Union football in Yorkshire (indeed in most parts of the country) is at the moment almost entirely a matter of improvisation. Some clubs are without grounds, some entirely without players, and everyone, without exception, greatly affected by wartime conditions. Nevertheless, the game continues and will continue wherever and whenever opportunity permits and its value, both as a relaxation from sterner duties and as a means to physical fitness was never more apparent.'*

It is difficult to understand why the Governing Bodies in rugby union made their initial announcements that seemed to indicate that no rugby would be played in wartime. There was an expectation that a war in 1939 would have much more impact on day to day life in Britain. The bombing of British towns and cities by the Germans, and also the spectre of gas attacks. In the First World War rugby union had continued to be played. However, much of that war was fought in the trenches in France and Belgium and air raids on British towns and cities were rare. Perhaps it was the expectation of a very different type of conflict that is the reason why the rugby authorities reacted in the way they did when the Second World War began

The early months of the Second World War were described as the 'Phoney War', a period given that title because, although the country was officially at war, very little fighting was actually taking place. Similarly, the first part of the 1939/40 season could be described as the 'Phoney Season' as, in the view of any rugby supporter observing the sport, it must have appeared to be 'business as usual.' Many clubs began to operate as they had pre-war. After the few opening games organised at short notice, Yorkshire clubs began in earnest to arrange their new fixture lists. As J.M. Kilburn remarks in his article in the Yorkshire Post on 20th September, *'The arrangement of fixtures according to normal principles is, of course, completely out of the question if only because the difficulties of travel preclude the undertaking of long journeys, and such matches as are to be played must presumably be on some sort of regional basis.'*

Clubs began to meet to plan fixtures. An example of this type of co-operation took place in Halifax where meetings were held at the White Swan Hotel in the town, in order for club officials to meet potential opponents and organise mutually convenient dates. At these meetings the host club Halifax was joined by Brighouse Rangers, Halifax Vandals, Halifax Collegians, Bradford Salem, Heath Old Boys, Old Crossleyans, Old Rishworthians and Old Brodleians with other clubs interested in the scheme invited to send a representative to future meetings.

1st Team HALIFAX 2nd Team

Date	*Opponents*	*At*	*Opponents*	*At*
Sep. 9	Morley	h	Morley 'A'	a
16	Otley	a	Otley 'A'	h
23	Brighouse Rangers	a	Huddfd. Old Boys 'A'	a
30	Fylde	a	Old Rishworthians	h
Oct. 7	Broughton Park	h	Broughton Park 'A'	a
14	Fylde	h	Old Crossleyans	a
21	Kendal	a	Huddfd. Old Boys 'A'	h
28	Roundhay	h	Roundhay 'A'	a
Nov. 4	Waterloo	h		
11	Wakefield	a	Wakefield 'A'	h
18	Sandal	h	Sandal 'A'	a
25	Old Roundhegians	a	Old Roundhegians 'A'	h
Dec. 2	Birkenhead Park	a	Roundhay	h
9	Harrogate Old Boys	h	Halifax Vandals	h
16	Manchester	h	Halifax Collegians	a
23	Bradford	h	Bradford 'A'	a
26	Brighouse Rangers	h		
30			Old Brodleians	h
Jan. 6	Cleckheaton	h	Cleckheaton 'A'	a
13	Waterloo	a	Old Crossleyans	h
20	Sale	h	Halifax Vandals	a
27	Roundhay	a	Heath Old Boys	h
Feb. 3	Bradford	a	Bradford 'A'	h
10	Birkenhead Park	h	Old Rishworthians	a
17	Wakefield	h	Wakefield 'A'	a
24	Sandal	a	Sandal 'A'	h
Mar. 2	Old Roundhegians	h	Old Roundhegians 'A'	a
9	Broughton Park	a	Broughton Park 'A'	h
16	Otley	h	Otley 'A'	a
23	EASTER HOLIDAY			
30	Morley	a	Morley 'A'	h
Apr. 6	Kendal	h		
13	Headingley	h	Headingley 'A'	a

Hon. Sec.—N. A. COLLINS, East Dene, Lea Avenue, Halifax (*Tel.* Day, 3447; Night, 2683).
Hon. Treas.—J. B. BARDSLEY, 3 Beechwood Villas, Halifax.
Captains—1st Team, D. HORSFOLD. 2nd Team, A. CROWTHER.
Ground—Ovenden Park. Bus from Commercial Street.
Dressing Rooms—Ovenden Park.
Headquarters—Ovenden Park.
Day and Time of Weekly Meeting—Tuesday, 8.15 p.m.
Club Colours—Blue and white.

191

The fixtures Halifax had planned to play in the 1939-40 season

Old Leodiensians, the Leeds based club, decided that their best way forward was to circulate their near neighbours in the hope of finding fixtures. The Old Leodiensians secretary wrote, *'We find we have a number of players still available, and I should be glad to fix up games if you are in a similar position. Distinction between 1st and 'A' will, I suppose, go by the board and it would be understood that cancellation at short notice or teams turning up short would be part of the inconvenience of war.'*

The Yorkshire Post also offered to help with arranging fixtures. J.M. Kilburn was anxious not to interfere with the arrangement of matches by club secretaries but he suggested that if clubs contacted the Yorkshire Post and indicated that they desired a fixture he would make sure that information was published so that clubs could be put in touch with each other. Mr Kilburn also offered this service to individual players looking for a game. A number of Yorkshire clubs had made it clear that they would not be attempting to re-start fixtures until the war was over and this obviously meant that there would be club less players wanting a game. Co-operation between clubs in order to provide games of rugby for any young men who wanted them became commonplace as the new season got into full swing.

Chapter Three

The Phoney Season

Following the stuttering start in mid September the 1939/40 season began in earnest. Many Yorkshire clubs found that they had sufficient players and officials in order to plan fixture lists for the first few months of the season. Others decided to play on a 'week to week' basis, agreeing a fixture only when they were sure of having fifteen players available. There were also clubs that did not make any attempt to arrange fixtures. Others that had initially planned to play fixtures discovered that the loss of many of their leading players meant that organising a representative team would be impossible. A notable early casualty of the war was Headingley, probably the strongest Yorkshire club in recent times. Headingley had arranged a fixture with Bradford on 30th September that did not take place and, as the season got underway, it looked as if Headingley would be one of the clubs not organising wartime rugby. However, the situation changed in November when on the 18th a Headingley team played an away game against St Peters School in York. This fixture was followed on the 25th November by a game against an Army team. The first club fixture played by Headingley in the 1939/40 season was against Otley away on Saturday 9th December. The game against Otley was described in the match report as the best game of the season. Unfortunately, although Headingley did have further fixtures planned for the New Year, these did not take place. It appears that Headingley's 1939/40 season consisted of just three games. There were a number of other clubs with a much lower profile than Headingley that did not organise fixtures in 1939. Batley, Bohemians and Nab Wood all

1st Team THE BOHEMIANS 2nd Team

Date	Opponents	At	Opponents	At
Sep. 9	Practice	h		
16	Practice	h		
23	R.A.F. (Dishforth)	h		
30	Moortown	a	Moortown 'A'	h
Oct. 7	Hull Ionians	h	Hull Ionians 'A'	a
14	Barnsley	a	Barnsley 'A'	h
21	Burley	h	Burley 'A'	a
28	Chirons	a	Chirons 'A'	h
Nov. 4	Moortown	h	Moortown 'A'	a
11	Selby	a	Selby 'A'	h
18	Old Morleians	h		
25	Sheffield University	a	Sheffield University 'A'	h
Dec. 2	Batley	h	Batley 'A'	a
9	Yarnbury	a		
16	Chirons	h	Chirons 'A'	a
23	Batley	a	Batley 'A'	h
30	Yarnbury	h	Yarnbury 'A'	a
Jan. 6	North Ribblesdale	h	North Ribblesdale 'A'	a
13	Selby	h	Selby 'A'	a
20	R.A.F. (Dishforth)	a		
27	Barnsley	h	Barnsley 'A'	a
Feb. 3	Old Leodiensians	a		
10				
17	Old Morleians	a		
24	North Ribblesdale	a	North Ribblesdale 'A'	h
Mar. 2	Leeds Salem	a	Leeds Salem 'A'	h
9	Wetherby	h	Wetherby 'A'	a
16	Hull Ionians	a	Hull Ionians 'A'	h
23	Leeds Salem	h	Leeds Salem 'A'	a
30				
Apr. 6	Bramley Old Boys	h	Bramley O.B. 'A'	a
13	Wetherby	a	Wetherby 'A'	h
20				

Hon. Sec.—W. D. Sharpe, 21 Barwick Road, Scholes (*Tel.* 28231).
Hon. Treas.—E. Binks, 147 Stanningley Road, Armley, Leeds (*Tel.* 30074).
Captain—C. D. Lea.
Ground—Waggon and Horses Hotel, Stanningley. Main Leeds-Bradford Road.
Dressing Rooms—At ground.
Headquarters—At ground.
Day and Time of Weekly Meeting—Training, Tuesdays and Thursdays, 7 p.m.
Club Colours—Royal blue and silver.
Result of Matches 1938-39—Played 25, won 10, lost 13, drawn 2. Points for, 250; against, 239.

170

Bohemians 1939-40 Fixture list – The last fixtures ever published by the club

had fixtures listed in the 1939/40 handbook but, apart from the one game Bohemians managed to play on the 2nd December 1939 against Leeds Salem, none of these clubs played during the war. For all three their final season ended in April 1939 as none of them were able to re-form after the war.

The revised fixture lists for the early part of the 1939/40 season were beginning to be announced. Bradford and Old Leodiensians were two clubs that had managed to arrange fixtures for both first and 'A' teams. Bradford started the season on the 23rd September with a practice match at its Lidget Green Ground. A Bradford fixture list was then announced featuring some of its traditional rivals such as Otley, Halifax and Roundhay.

Bradford

Sept	**30th**	**Old Leodiensians**	**Home**
Oct	**7th**	**Halifax**	**Home**
	14th	**Otley**	**Away**
	21st	**Halifax**	**Away**
	28th	**Otley**	**Home**

Nov	4th	Morley	Home
	11th	Morley	Away
	18th	Roundhay	Home
	25th	Harrogate O.B.	Away
Dec	2nd	Old Leodiensians	Away
	9th	Harrogate O.B.	Home
	16th	Roundhay	Away

Old Leodiensians were due to play clubs such as Sandal and Morley in a fixture list that covered the period from October to December. Old Leodiensians had also managed to organise fixtures against Bradford's first team. This arrangement that would not have happened before the war, as Bradford would only play its 'A' or Extra 1st XV against Leodiensians. In fact in their home fixture against Bradford, Old Leodiensians lost by 8 points to 3, giving what was described in the match report as their best display of the season.

Old Leodiensians

Sept	30th	Bradford	Away
Oct	7th	Sandal	Home
	14th	Morley	Home
	21st	Sandal	Away
	28th	Morley	Away
Nov	4th	Medical School	Home
	11th	Roundhay	Home
	18th	--------------	
	25th	Medical School	Away
Dec	2nd	Bradford	Home
	9th	Roundhay	Home

Many clubs, it appeared, were just happy to have a fixture and the old 'pecking orders' were largely forgotten as they looked out for opponents that would be able find fifteen players on a Saturday and so be able to fulfil the fixture. The other problem for some clubs was that they often did not know exactly which players were going to be available until the day of a game. Leave arrangements for men in the forces could be changed at the last minute and sometimes, because of the travel restrictions, players would be unable to get back home in time for the game.

In the early weeks of the 'Phoney Season' many clubs, both senior and junior, began to organise fixtures against other clubs and also games against Services teams. In fact it was Services teams that seemed to 'kick start' the season. In 1938/39 there were six Services clubs in membership of the Yorkshire RFU. The majority of these were RAF Stations but, for many clubs in September and October 1939, it was local Army units that raised teams and provided fixtures. Otley began their season with a fixture against a Services team that included a number of players who had often been seen in Otley's colours. Otley, who usually charged admission for their home games, decided that for

1st Team HUDDERSFIELD OLD BOYS 2nd Team

Date	*Opponents*	*At*	*Opponents*	*At*
Sep. 16	Batley	a	Batley 'A'	h
23	Old Hymerians	h	Halifax 'A'	h
30	Wakefield	a	Wakefield 'A'	h
Oct. 7	Hull and E.R.	a	Halifax Vandals	a
14	Scarborough	a		
21	Hull and E.R.	h	Halifax 'A'	a
28	Headingley	h	Headingley 'A'	a
Nov. 4	Otley	a	Otley 'A'	h
11	Tyldesley	a	Old Crossleyans	h
18	Sale	h	Ashtonians	a
25	Leicester Stoneygate	h	English Electric	a
Dec. 2	Morley	a	Morley 'A'	h
9	Broughton Park	a	Broughton Park 'A'	h
16	Barnsley	h	Huddersfield Y.M.C.A.	a
23	Harrogate Old Boys	h	Saddleworth	a
26	Roundhay	a		
30	Batley	h	Batley 'A'	a
Jan. 6	Wakefield	h	Wakefield 'A'	a
13	Bradford	a	Bradford 'A'	h
20	Heaton Moor	h	Heaton Moor 'A'	a
27	St. Helens	h	Nab Wood	a
Feb. 3	Old Edwardians	h	Old Rishworthians	h
10	Heaton Moor	a	Heaton Moor 'A'	h
17	Broughton Park	h	Broughton Park 'A'	a
24	Scarborough	h	Bradford Salem	a
Mar. 2	Wigan Old Boys	a	Sheffield University	h
9	Bradford	h	Bradford 'A'	a
16	Roundhay	h	Roundhay 'A'	a
23–25	Tour to Lake District			
30	Skipton	h	Skipton 'A'	a
Apr. 6	Sheffield	a	Sheffield 'A'	h
13	Ilkley	a	Roundhay 'A'	h

Hon. Sec.—W. A. Scott, Longwood House, Fixby, Huddersfield. *Hon. Fixt. Sec.*—J. B. Sugden, 6 Heaton Road, Gledholt, Huddersfield (*Tel.* Home, 1278; Business, Honley 75). *Hon. Treas.*—J. A. Bottomley, 5 Westfield Avenue, Oakes, Huddersfield; J. C. V. Grundy, 61 Heaton Road, Gledholt, Huddersfield (*Tel.* 2016).
Captains—1st Team, George H. Shore. 2nd Team, Peter Lockwood.
Ground—Waterloo (*Tel.* 1663). Trolley bus from Westgate or Lepton bus from Lord Street.
Dressing Rooms—On ground.
Headquarters—George Hotel, (*Tel.* 3271 or 3282).
Day and Time of Weekly Meeting—Monday, 7.30 p.m. at Headquarters.
Club Colours—White jersey with claret and gold band; white knickers.

207

The fixtures Huddersfield Old Boys had planned to play in the 1939-40 season

this first game of the season that there would be no admission charge for members of the Forces who attended in uniform. Huddersfield Old Boys also began their season with a fixture against a local Army unit.

As the Universities and Colleges returned from their summer break, they also provided fixtures for the clubs in search of opponents. In Sheffield and Hull, fixtures against the local University meant that there were no major travel problems to overcome. Also, because the University team was made up of students, there was less chance of a last minute cancellation, as happened on occasions with Services teams. Headingley Old Boys, one of the stronger Leeds junior clubs, did not initially organise fixtures for 1939/40 but decided to hold 'scratch games' at their ground every Saturday afternoon at 3.00 pm and extended an invitation to any players who had difficulty in finding a game to go along. All the players who attended were guaranteed to play, as, if there were more than thirty players at the ground, changes would be made at half time in order to ensure everyone was able to take part. David Duncan, the President and acting Secretary and Treasurer of Headingley Old Boys, stated in an article in the Yorkshire Post on 23rd September that, '*We are not asking them to join our club, or pay a subscription; we are simply offering them a chance of a game.*' By the end of October the situation at Headingley Old Boys changed. There were many more Army teams wanting matches and more and more clubs were looking for fixtures so the Old Boys decided to arrange regular fixtures. A meeting was held on Monday 30th October at which Headingley Old Boys, Burley and Yarnbury agreed to a wartime amalgamation under the name of Headingley Old Boys. Yarnbury were unable to play any wartime fixtures. This was because huts to house the workers from the AVRO factory at Yeadon had been built on the Yarnbury pitch after it had been requisitioned by the RAF. As a result of the formal amalgamation, Headingley Old Boys were hoping to turn out two teams every week.

The Halifax District had led the way in organising regular fixtures with officials from the Halifax club being the driving forces. In the early weeks of the season most of the Halifax clubs had played fixtures against Army XVs and other local clubs; some even managed to arrange fixture lists up to Christmas. The Halifax District clubs continued to meet to discuss fixtures but Halifax was not the only part of Yorkshire where the 'Phoney Season' began in earnest. Clubs in all the three Ridings of Yorkshire began to organise regular games and by early December over sixty, more than half the clubs in membership of the Yorkshire RFU, had been 'in action,' some just playing occasional games, while others were playing a fixture every week, and in some cases turning out two teams. In Hull, it was the Hull and East Riding club and Old Hymerians that led the way. Hull and East Riding made an announcement in the Hull Daily Mail, on 20th September 1939 that their fixtures for 1939/40 season were cancelled. The statement added that they hoped to be able to play some friendly fixtures but that they would like players to contact the secretary if they were available to play. The appeal for players was successful and a programme of weekly fixtures in Hull began in early October!

Jim Brough

Roundhay's season began on 7th October in rather controversial circumstances. On Wednesday 4th October Roundhay's team for their home fixture against an Army XV was published in the Yorkshire Post with Jim Brough, the former Leeds Rugby League international, listed at full-back.

On the following day, the 5th October, it was reported in the same newspaper that Jim Brough was not going to be allowed to play. In the article he wrote about the situation J.M. Kilburn, the Post's rugby union correspondent, expressed surprise at the ruling. Mr Kilburn assumed that as the Rugby Football Union and the majority of regional unions had formally abandoned their playing commitments, then the rules regarding rugby league players taking part in rugby union football would be relaxed.

To support his belief, Mr Kilburn quoted the situation in the First World War when rugby league players were welcomed in rugby union. Despite the protests, Jim Brough did not play with Roundhay and in fact returned to Leeds to play rugby league again. It was to be another five weeks before the Rugby Football Union clarified the situation regarding rugby league players. In Chapters Eleven and Twelve I will discuss the relationship between the two codes and the impact of situations like the one that arose when Jim Brough was asked to play for Roundhay.

Most of the clubs that had re-started were able to find Services teams to augment their fixture lists, and there were even some school teams that provided opposition for clubs keen to provide their players with regular games of rugby. The impact on clubs of men being called up meant that the teams fielded often included young players who had just left school and as a result many of the games against school teams were very even contests. The 1939/40 season was in full swing by the middle of October with Bradford being described in the Yorkshire Post by J.M. Kilburn as, '*in magnificent form just now and even if we assume some wartime weakness among their opponents there can be no doubting the quality of the Bradford play.*'

H. Anderson Roundhay's captain for the 1939-40 season

On 21st October in the Yorkshire Post J.M. Kilburn commented that, '*Playing sport and watching games form important safety valves for national feelings and it is clear more and more people are appreciating the recreative effects as the weeks go by.*'

By December 1939, the season was certainly providing much more rugby than anyone could possibly have anticipated when the first tentative fixtures had been organised in late September. Some clubs were playing every Saturday while others were still organising fixtures at short notice when they were sure that they would have fifteen players available. There were surprising results in fixtures where the fifteen players fielded by some clubs would vary greatly week to week. Results like Ossett beating Roundhay were becoming common as some clubs were often unable to name a team until the players arrived at the ground on a Saturday afternoon. However, towards the end of December, nature and not war began to have an even bigger impact on the 'Phoney Season'. One of the longest and snowiest winters of the century meant that fixtures ground to a halt at the beginning of January 1940. Censorship also meant that there were few headlines in the newspapers about this winter, one that has been described as the worst for forty five years. Savage cold and heavy snow with deep drifting covered the country. Places like Sheffield reported four foot drifts in late January. It was not until early February that temperatures began to rise and the snow and ice that caused massive transport disruption began to thaw.

The terrible winter seemed to affect many of the County's clubs and for some the 1939/40 season ended in December 1939. Perhaps the sustained period of bad weather and the increasing number of players being called up for active service drained the enthusiasm of some of the clubs that had re-started in October and November. By the end of 1939 more than 1.5 million men had been conscripted to join the British armed forces. Whatever the reason, there were fewer clubs in action in late February 1940 when games resumed than there had been in November and early December 1939. During January and early February some clubs did announce fixtures in the hope that there would be a sudden dramatic improvement in the weather but no games took place. In fact the weather was so severe that newspapers like the Yorkshire Post announced that they would no longer publish lists of postponed games. Presumably the assumption was made that anyone venturing out into the arctic weather would know that there was no likely hood of outdoor sporting fixtures taking place. It is difficult to speculate about what might have happened to clubs and fixtures in 1939/40 if the winter weather had not been so extreme. By January 1940 the war was beginning to have much more of an impact on everyday life and it is possible that more club mergers and amalgamations would have taken place. Some clubs may have decided that, as there were opportunities for many of their members to play in Services teams, the increasingly difficult task of finding fifteen players and opponents who were also able to find raise a team meant that it was better close down until the end of hostilities.

Chapter Four

After the Freeze

It was the 24th February 1940 before rugby union fixtures could re-start in Yorkshire. The terrible winter had hit all outdoor sports very hard. Some rugby union fixtures were played on Boxing Day 1939 and after the resumption in activity in October and November hopes will have been high that the start of 1940 would see the majority of clubs able to continue to organise fixtures. Unfortunately, once the weather eased and the season re-started, it appeared that some of the post Christmas enthusiasm had been dissipated. The fixtures that had been organised during the 'big freeze' in the hope of a quick thaw did not, of course, take place. An example was Halifax arranging to play Otley on 10th February. This fixture would have been one of the highlights of the season. A few clubs managed to play fixtures on the 24th February but it was those that had been quick off the mark in September and October, organising fixture lists rather than planning games 'week to week' that returned to action. Clubs like Roundhay, Huddersfield Old Boys and Bradford had obviously retained enough players and officials so that they were in a position to respond quickly once the temperatures warmed up.

The 1939/40 season could easily have petered out with clubs deciding to close down for the season and attempting to regroup in September 1940. The fact that the rugby activity did continue was possibly down to two main factors. One was the extension of the season until the 30th April. This decision was made by the RFU so that clubs could play more games and ease their financial worries. Finances were a big factor for clubs that owned their own grounds, and a few extra fixtures may have been an incentive for some to continue playing until the end of April. The second factor in Yorkshire was the organisation of a wartime knockout cup competition. The competition was proposed by Captain Stanley J. Rhodes from the Bradford club. A meeting of interested clubs on the 15th February agreed that, subject to approval from the Yorkshire RFU, the competition would take place. It was hoped that the wartime cup would generate funds for the clubs that took part. A percentage of all the gate receipts were to be pooled and then shared. It was also proposed that at every game a collection would be taken, with the proceeds given to the Red Cross. The wartime cup competition was approved by the Yorkshire RFU. Sixteen clubs entered and the draw was made on the 1st March at the Midland Hotel in Bradford. The clubs taking part were all West Riding based. The travel restrictions and petrol rationing probably ruled out clubs like Hull and East Riding and Sheffield even though both would have expected to be very competitive.

The draw for the first round was:

Sandal v Huddersfield Old Boys

Morley v Bingley

Keighlians v Skipton

Bradford v Bradford Salem

Otley v Ossett

Brighouse Rangers v Roundhay

Halifax v Halifax Vandals

Harrogate Old Boys v Baildon

The first round of the competition was scheduled for Saturday 9th March. Bradford would have been everyone's favourites to lift the trophy as, in the early part of the season, they had been the strongest and most successful club in Yorkshire. There was no pressure on clubs to enter. Presumably those that did enter were the ones that felt they could turn out a representative team and travel if they were drawn away. It may even have been a competition that was restricted to the first sixteen clubs to express interest. A restricted entry would mean that the competition could be completed before the end of the season. Old Leodiensians and Headingley Old Boys had been playing regular fixtures but did not take part in the knockout cup. Both may have made the decision not to enter because they were struggling for player numbers after the long break. In fact, on the 2nd March the fixture between the two was played with only thirteen players on each side, before Christmas both clubs had been turning out two teams on a regular basis.

Skipton's XV for their 1st Round Cup game against Keighlians

The cup competition produced some surprises, none more so than Brighouse Rangers victory by 6 points to nil against Roundhay. Roundhay had been having a good season; they regularly had sufficient players for two teams and had won a majority of the games played before Christmas. They would have begun the cup competition as one of the favourites to reach the final. For Brighouse, the cup provided a big boost for the club and the town. In the second round the Rangers played Halifax, another club that expected to have a successful cup run. Another shock result saw Brighouse win by 11 points to nil. The semi final was to be played on a home and away basis and, as their opponents were Otley, it was widely expected in rugby circles that Brighouse's cup run would come to an end at the semi final stage. The first leg of the semi final was played at Brighouse Rangers Lane Head Ground and produced an attendance of over 1,500. Brighouse won the first leg by 9 points to nil. In the second leg at Cross Green, Otley's ground, an attendance of over 2,000 spectators saw Brighouse lose by 9 points to 3 in a game that Otley had been expected to win easily and so make up the deficit from the first leg. However, it was not to be Brighouse qualified for the final, winning by 12 points to 9 on aggregate. Bradford, as widely expected, were Brighouse Rangers opponents in the final. Bradford had beaten Bradford Salem in the first round by 62 points to 3. In the second round they played another local derby, this time against Keighlians. This game was played at Lawkholme Lane, the home ground of Keighley Rugby League Club and, Bradford won by 41 points to nil. In the semi final Bradford faced Sandal, another club that was in good form during the cup competition. In the first round Sandal had beaten Huddersfield Old Boys by 18 points to nil. This was another shock result, as Huddersfield had won their previous fifteen games. However, in the semi final Sandal were brought down to earth by Bradford who, over two legs, won fairly comfortably with an aggregate score of 21 points to 7.

The final of the wartime knockout cup was scheduled for Saturday 20th April 1940, another Rugby League Ground, Odsal Stadium, the home of Bradford Northern, was the venue. In Brighouse, the appearance of their local team in the final of a cup competition revived memories of forty five years earlier when in 1895 Brighouse Rangers appeared in the final of the Yorkshire Cup. As the 20th April approached, the enthusiasm for the game in Brighouse increased dramatically. The Brighouse Echo built up the excitement in its preview articles. Comparisons between the 1895 Rangers team and the 1940 team were made. Pen pictures of the Brighouse players were published and the newspaper expected that several thousand Brighouse supporters would be making the short journey to Odsal Stadium.

As an 8 year old, Philip Dearnaly was taken to Odsal by his father to watch Brighouse Rangers play Bradford in the Cup Final. He had never been to a rugby match before and in fact his father was a soccer supporter who followed Huddersfield Town. Philip recalls catching the coach at Waterloo near the Brighouse Ground. This was another 'first' as Philip had never been on a coach before. He recalls that he was amazed by the crowd and atmosphere at Odsal. Philip thought that his father who worked at the Dye Works in Brighouse knew one of the players, possibly at stoker at the Dye Works. That, plus the euphoria in the town, encouraged him to go to the game which produced one of the largest attendances ever for a rugby union cup final in Yorkshire. There were 9,442 spectators at Odsal that day with receipts of over £500. Unfortunately, Brighouse Rangers cup run came to an end in the final as Bradford won the game by 22 points to 3. There was disappointment in Brighouse regarding the result, but a great deal of pride in their team of largely unknown local players who had given such a boost to the town by their stirring cup performances.

Harrogate Old Boys and Huddersfield Old Boys, two of the clubs that had been defeated in the early stages of the competition recovered from the cup disappointment and continued to play regular fixtures until the end of the season. Huddersfield had lost 18 points to nil at Sandal in the first round, while Harrogate beat Baildon 13 points to 3 in the first round and then lost in the second round by 33 points to nil against Otley. The cup results in full are:

1st round

Sandal 18 Huddersfield Old Boys

Morley 20 Bingley 0

Keighlians 8 Skipton 6

Bradford 62 Bradford Salem 3

Otley 26 Ossett 0

Brighouse Rangers 6 Roundhay 0

Halifax 27 Halifax Vandals 6

Harrogate Old Boys 13 Baildon 3

2nd round

Sandal 13 Morley 3

Bradford 41 Keighlians 0

Otley 33 Harrogate Old Boys 0

Brighouse Rangers 11 Halifax 3

Semi finals

1st leg

Brighouse Rangers 9 Otley 0

Sandal 0 Bradford 12

2nd leg

Otley 9 Brighouse Rangers 3

Bradford 9 Sandal 7

Final

Bradford 22 Brighouse Rangers 3

Odsal Stadium again played host to Yorkshire rugby union clubs when, on Saturday the 27th April, a seven a side competition was held at the ground. Eight clubs entered the sevens and Bradford again proved the strongest team, beating Otley in the final by 15 points to 5. Another good attendance was recorded for the event with over 1,400 spectators contributing more than £66 in gate receipts. Another sevens competition was held in Hull on the same day when eleven teams took part in the event, the proceeds of which were to be shared between the Eric Winkley Memorial Fund and the Hull Minesweeper Fund. The sevens was won by an RAF team that defeated Old Hymerians in the final by 16 points to nil. Seven a side competitions were the traditional way in which in the rugby union season ended, but few people back in September 1939 would have expected the 1939/40 season to end with a cup final and sevens competitions.

Although the 1939/40 season had a traditional end it had been far from a normal season. After the resumption of fixtures in February, there were far fewer clubs playing regular games. Some of the clubs that had managed to play a few games prior to Christmas, such as Headingley, West Leeds Old Boys and Old Brodleians, obviously decided it was time to close down until the end of hostilities. Player movement between clubs was now common practice and so any players looking for a game on a Saturday afternoon generally had few problems in finding a club willing to accommodate them. Looking back on the season, it is possible to reflect that after such a chaotic beginning with lots of very mixed official messages being given by the authorities it is remarkable that so much rugby was played. At their Annual General Meeting held on 27th May 1940 twenty Baildon members heard a very positive report on the 1939/40 season from the first team Secretary Mr H. Kitson. He reported that despite the terrible winter twenty one fixtures had been played. Baildon also reported a profit for the season of £19 12s 6d, this was despite the majority of the fund raising events such as the Annual Dinner having to be postponed. What would the 1940/41 season bring? By the end of April 1940 the war was having a much bigger impact. The 'Phoney War' of late 1939 and early 1940 had come to an end and life was going to be very difficult as the fighting intensified in Europe and the serious bombing of British cities began. How would rugby union survive in these very difficult times?

Chapter Five

1940 -1942

1940/41

On the 20th September 1940 representatives of over thirty clubs met at the Metropole Hotel in Leeds to discuss fixture arrangements for the new season. Remarkably, considering what had happened during the summer, one of those clubs was Roundhay. The North Leeds based club was dealt a massive blow when, in summer 1940, its clubhouse was burnt to the ground. Despite the fire, officials made an appeal in the Yorkshire Post on 24th August 1940 for any players who had no other means of playing, particularly young ones, to contact them. Roundhay also announced that training was to begin on Tuesday 10th September. By the time the club played its opening fixture of the season on the 21st September against Old Leodiensians, a remarkable effort by the members meant that most of the damage caused by the fire had been repaired and the Chandos Park ground was ready to host games. In the 1939/40 season, Roundhay had played thirty eight games, more than they had ever played in one season. However, the reality was that the thirty eight included games played by a 'second' team that was, on most weeks, as strong as the first team. Of the thirty eight games Roundhay played in 1939/40 thirteen were won, twenty three lost and there were two draws. One club that was not able to continue was Heath Old Boys. The Halifax based club was one of a number that had their pitch requisitioned and ploughed up. Sheffield Tigers was another. They had managed to play a few fixtures in the 1939/40 season but once they lost their pitch the club had to close down.

The rugby union season in Yorkshire had in fact begun on Wednesday 11th September when Baildon played the Duke of Wellington's Regiment, with a return fixture held a week later at Otley. Baildon had become a centre for rugby in the North of Bradford. The club was able to regularly turn out two teams, often encouraging Servicemen on leave to play for the club. As the number of clubs continuing to play declined, there were more like Baildon providing an opportunity for a game of rugby to anyone, regardless of who they had played for. If a player appeared at a ground with boots and kit, he was likely to be offered a game.

After their success in reaching the final of the wartime cup competition, Brighouse Rangers decided that as they still had twelve of the 1939/40 team available they were going to be able to carry on. According to the Brighouse Chronicle, they relied on other rugby men from the district to make up their team. Halifax and Huddersfield Old Boys also got back into action during September. On Saturday 28th September a new name appeared on the rugby scene in Yorkshire. A team called Octurians played against a combined Ilkley/Otley XV. I assume that Octurians was the name given to the Officer Cadet Training Unit (O.C.T.U.) that was based in Ilkley. Octurians continued to play regular fixtures with Stacks Field, at Ilkley, their home ground. The other clubs that announced fixture lists for 1940/41 included Sandal, Hull and East Riding and Harrogate Old Boys.

The opportunity for players to play wherever there was a fixture taking place was officially sanctioned by Bob Oakes, who in a letter to the Yorkshire clubs said, *'There are any number of Rugger players in different districts in the county, all of whom will not be engaged by their Service side who will be delighted to have the chance of a few games. Every possible effort should be made to get in touch with the Service units in your locality.'* Clubs were operating as they had in 1939/40. Some, like Huddersfield Old Boys, Baildon and Skipton, planned fixtures for the season while others like York, Leeds YMCA and Cleckheaton organised fixtures when they were sure of having fifteen players available.

Old Roundhegians decided to re-start in September 1940. The club had closed down in 1939 as the committee had resigned and their pitch was no longer available. In August 1940 a group of old boys of Roundhay School met to discuss the possibility of running an Old Roundhegians team during the forthcoming season. After a discussion it was decided that it was not a practical proposition, but then a month later the group met again and reconsidered. After the second meeting, training sessions were held and two games were organised against the school. Old Roundhegians lost both games and the organisers were very pessimistic about continuing. However, during October and the early part of November more players appeared, fixtures were organised and on 16th November Old Roundhegians recommenced the season. Fixtures against Baildon 'A', Old Hilmians, Harrogate Old Boys and Old Leodiensians were included in a list that gave the club regular games right through to the end of March 1941. It is not clear whether Old Roundhegians did manage to continue to play after 1941. The close proximity of Roundhay, who were often able to organise two teams, must have tempted some Old Roundhegians players to move to Chandos Park.

Odsal Stadium again staged a rugby union match when on 16th November 1940 Yorkshire played Lancashire. Lancashire won the game playing in Yorkshire's white jerseys by 22 points to 10. An attendance of 3,500 produced receipts of £180 from which £130 was donated to the Red Cross. The return fixture was played at Central Park, the home of Wigan Rugby League Club, on 8th March 1940. The Yorkshire team that won that game by 15 points to 8 contained ten rugby league players. An attendance of 6,000 raised £300 for the Red Cross. These representative fixtures were the forerunners of a number of this type of game that took place in Yorkshire during the war. Some of these games were organised by Bob Oakes and some by the Northern Command Sports Board. All of these fixtures attracted good attendances and as a result various charities received donations from the gate receipts.

In late November Bob Oakes wrote to all the Yorkshire clubs to ask whether they would support a 1940/41 wartime cup competition. The 1939/40 cup had been a big success and if the clubs agreed to a 1940/41 competition it was planned to be played in the New Year and over six weeks, so as not to disrupt the fixtures that had already been organised.

Clubs were informed that the proposal to hold a wartime cup was to be discussed at a County Committee meeting on 17th December 1940. When the Yorkshire Committee met it was agreed, following consultation, that there would not be a wartime cup in 1940/41 as there were insufficient clubs interested. Many, including Halifax and Otley, two of the strongest, were happy with the local fixtures they had arranged. The restrictions on travel could have meant some clubs may have found it difficult, if not impossible, to play in a cup game that involved a journey of any distance outside their own local area. The idea of playing a wartime cup, in Yorkshire was not considered again by the County, and so Bradford retained the trophy that they won in April 1940.

However, there was some positive news to come out of the meeting on 17th December and that was that twenty four clubs in addition to the Services XVs were playing regular fixtures, with one or two additions likely to join in shortly. This number was about a third the number that had played in 1939/40 but it was a figure that remained fairly constant over the next two years. This was despite the fact that the war was now having a massive impact on everyday life. Bombing raids with devastating effects were taking place across Yorkshire with places such as Hull, Leeds and Sheffield suffering particularly badly. In fact Goddard Avenue, where Hull and East Riding played, had been bombed in February 1940 with a number of casualties reported.

An interesting representative fixture took place on the 15th February 1941 at Odsal Stadium when a Yorkshire Services XV played a Challenge match against a Northern Command XV.

The proceeds from the fixture were donated to Army charities. Both teams contained a number of international rugby league players from both England and Wales and some of the leading rugby union players that were stationed in the North of England. In the match programme it was suggested that in fact the Northern Command of the British Army possessed the best set of rugby players to be found anywhere in the British Isles. The Northern Command XV won the game by 17 points to 5, over 5,000 spectators were present and the Army charities received £200 from the gate receipts. The stars of the game were two rugby league internationals, Gus Risman and Stanley Brogden.

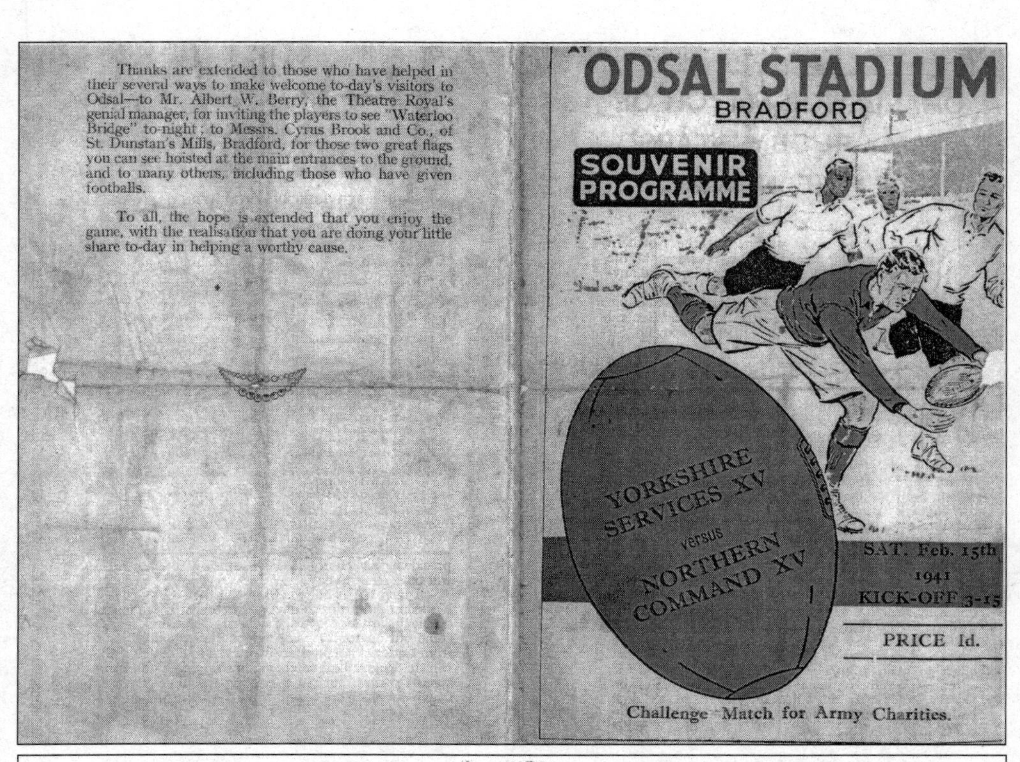

Thanks are extended to those who have helped in their several ways to make welcome to-day's visitors to Odsal—to Mr. Albert W. Berry, the Theatre Royal's genial manager, for inviting the players to see "Waterloo Bridge" to-night; to Messrs. Cyrus Brook and Co., of St. Dunstan's Mills, Bradford, for those two great flags you can see hoisted at the main entrances to the ground, and to many others, including those who have given footballs.

To all, the hope is extended that you enjoy the game, with the realisation that you are doing your little share to-day in helping a worthy cause.

CHALLENGE MATCH OF ARMY RUGBY 'STARS' OF THE NORTH.

By the Editor

IT is the belief of many people that the Northern Command of the British Army possesses at the moment the best set of Rugby players to be found anywhere in these Isles.

Those talented players are paired at Odsal Stadium to-day in a match under the patronage of the General Officer Commanding in Chief, Northern Command, Sir Robert Adam, Bart.

Players of the two branches of Rugby, League and Union, have been combined to provide the rivalry wherein Captain G. Gourlay's powerful Catterick Garrison team has been so strengthened as a Yorkshire Services XV. that has challenged a side chosen from the rest of the Command.

For Army Charities.

What better place to hold such a match than Odsal, whose Rugby attendances have on six occasions this season been the biggest on the particular Saturday at any football match in the country, as is, of course, only befitting the ground on which the Rugby League champions play? And for what better purpose to stage such a match than Army charities?

All the League players appearing here to-day could have appeared with their clubs, probably receiving monetary payment. The Union players could, no doubt, have had a game nearer their temporary homes without the necessity of having to travel to Bradford. Instead, they have all rallied enthusiastically to the cause and in the spirit of the challenge in a voluntary effort to make a success of this day. With similar enthusiasm and voluntary effort, Mr. Harry Hornby, Odsal's hon. managing director, has done his part, realising that the Army's best Rugby talent deserves the full co-operation of Rugby's most successful Club.

In the cause of sport and charity, Odsal Stadium's management will never be found wanting in any demands which the Northern Command or the Army authorities may wish to bring forward, and in this there is ready welcome and support from Odsal's esteemed

To-day's Team Line-up.

YORKSHIRE SERVICES XV	NORTHERN COMMAND XV
Colours: Blue and Yellow Jerseys Blue Shorts.	Colours: Green Jerseys, White Shorts.
1 Pte. J. Kelly (Leeds)	1 Cpl. J. Miller (Hull) *cb*
2 Capt. Lees (Halifax) capt.	2 Lieut. G. Blamire (Heriots)
3 L/Cpl. D. Case (Bradford Nor.) *a*	3 Cpl. S. Brogden (Hull) *cb*
4 L/Cpl. W. Davies (Huddersfield)	4 Cpl. J. Risman (Salford) *a*
5 Cpl. L. Lloyd (Castleford) *a*	5 Dvr. V. Rhydderch (Oldham)
6 Pte. Hurcombe (Halifax)	6 Pte. W. G. Morgan (Huddersfield)
7 L/Cpl. Booth (Hunslet)	7 Srgt. O. Morris (Leeds) *a*
8 Sigmn. W. Western (Bedford) *b*	8 Gnr. G. Prosser (Leeds) *a*
9 L/Cpl. J. Dandy (Otley) *b*	9 Pte. Duke (Hull)
10 Cadet Hoskyn (Rosslyn Park)	10 Cadet Bowen (Worcestershire)
11 Cadet R. Dunbar (Glasgow Unv.) *b*	11 Srgt. Simpson (Huddersfield)
12 Sigmn. K. Jubb (Leeds) *cb*	12 Pte. Lowe (Hull)
13 Cpl. E. Tattersfield (Leeds) *cb*	13 Srgt. J. Thompson (Headingley)
14 L/Cpl. G. Brown (Batley) *b*	14 Capt. J. Rowlands (Durham)
15 Cpl. T. Foster (Bradford Nor.) *a*	15 L/Cpl. C. Whitehead (Hunslet) *a*
Reserve: Pilot Officer T. F. Dorward (Gala and Scotland) and Pte. Warn (Devon County)	*c Played for England* *b Played for Yorkshire* *a Played for Wales*

Referee: H. Athorne (Yorkshire County.)
Touch-Judges F. Ayres (Hon. Sec., Yorkshire R. U. Referees Society)
H. A. S. Malir (Yorkshire R. U. Committee)

president, Sir Henry P. Price, who, with Lady Price, will be present to-day.

Irrespective of whether Captain G. Gourlay's Yorkshire side wins to-day, or whether it is the fortune of Lieutenant F. Lloyd's Northern Command side to come out on top, a challenge has been jointly issued from Catterick to Bradford Northern to a match if they win the Rugby League championship. Should circumstances permit, but not forgetting the more important match in which we have all got to be on the winning side, the match will be arranged.

Match Programme

On the same afternoon in February Sandal, Roundhay and Baildon all played fixtures but an indication of some of the difficulties faced in early 1941 was that for the fixture between Otley and Headingley Old Boys both clubs could only raise fourteen players.

Towards the end of the season news about the rugby union scene in Yorkshire and reports on games became more difficult to find in newspapers like the Yorkshire Post. Newsprint restrictions meant that newspapers could often only report on the progress of the war and the professional sports such as soccer that continued to be played. As there was no cup competition to provide a climax to the season, the fixtures ended as usual in mid April. I imagine that clubs that managed to complete the season, despite all the adversity, will have considered it a huge success. Roundhay were not able to play as many games as in 1939/40 but still recorded a very respectable twenty one fixtures, with eleven wins, seven losses and three draws. The annual seven a side competitions were becoming more difficult to organise but on 26th April 1941 a sixteen team sevens competition did take place at Otley, with the proceeds again being donated to local charities. Amongst the clubs that fielded teams were Brighouse Rangers, Halifax, Huddersfield Old Boys, Roundhay, Baildon and the hosts Otley. Those clubs were joined by a number of Services teams. In the final, Baildon defeated Brighouse by 6 points to nil. Otley had not played many fixtures during the 1940/41 season and the sevens competition was probably the last club rugby to be played at Cross Green until September 1945.

1941/42

A Yorkshire clubs meeting was held in September 1941, the main purpose of which was to discuss fixtures for the season. It was also a good opportunity for secretaries to fill in any blanks they had in their fixture lists. The new season for most clubs began on Saturday 20th September. Huddersfield Old Boys and Halifax, both of whom had managed to organise full fixture lists, were amongst the first back into action. Roundhay had actually begun their season a week earlier when they travelled to Baildon and won by 8 points to 3. To begin their season, Baildon had played a midweek fixture at Ilkley on Wednesday 10th September against an O.C.T.U. XV.

FIXTURES, 1941/42.

Date	Club	Gd.	R.	SCORE Baildon Gl	Tr	Pt	Oppon'ts Gl	Tr	Pt
1941									
Aug. 30									
Sept. 6									
,, 10	O.C.T.U., Ilkley	H							
,, 13	Roundhay	H							
,, 17	R.A.F., Yeadon	H							
,, 20	Skipton	A							
,, 24	R.A.F., Yeadon	H							
,, 27	Hudds. O.B.	H							
Oct. 4	Eng. Electric	A							
,, 11	Leeds Univers.	A							
,, 18	9th F'ld T. Reg.	H							
,, 25	Hudds. O.B.	A							
Nov. 1	Leeds Medicals	H							
,, 8	Halifax	A							
,, 15	Sandal	H							
,, 22	Skipton	H							
,, 29	Leeds Medicals	A							
Dec. 6	Middlesex Hosp.	A							
,, 13	Halifax	H							
,, 20	Sandal	A							
,, 27	Harrogate O.B.	H							
1942									
Jan. 3	O.C.T.U., Ilkley	A							
,, 10	Headingley O.B.	H							
,, 17	Keighley O.B.	H							
,, 24	Brighouse	H							
,, 31	Headingley O.B.	A							
Feb. 7	O.C.T.U., Ilkley	H							
,, 14	Brighouse	A							
,, 21	Keighlians	H							
,, 28	R.A.F., Ch. Fn.	H							
Mar. 7	Eng. Electric	H							
,, 14	Roundhay	A							
,, 21	Keighley O.B.	H							
,, 28	Harrogate O.B.	A							
April 4	Catterick Garr.	H							
,, 11	Keighlians	A							
,, 18									
,, 25									

FIXTURES, 1941/42.

Date	Club	Gd.	R.	SCORE Baildon Gl	Tr	Pt	Oppon'ts Gl	Tr	Pt
1941									
Aug. 30									
Sept. 6									
,, 10									
,, 13									
,, 17									
,, 20	Keighley O.B.	H							
,, 24									
,, 27									
Oct. 4									
,, 11	D. of Well. Hx.	H							
,, 18	Army XV.	A							
,, 25	Bfd. Tech. Coll.	H							
Nov. 1	D. of Well. Hx.	A							
,, 8	Keighley O.B.	H							
,, 15	Headingley O.B.	A							
,, 22	Coll. of Res'n.	A							
,, 29	Coll. of Res'n.	H							
Dec. 6	O.C.T.U. Res'n	H							
,, 13	Bradford Tech.	A							
,, 20	Army XV.	H							
,, 27	Army XV.	A							
1942									
Jan. 3	Headingley O.B.	H							
,, 10	Leeds Med. 'A'	A							
,, 17	O.C.T.U. "A"	A							
,, 24									
,, 31	Middx. Hos. 'A'	H							
Feb. 7									
,, 14	Keighley O.B.	H							
,, 21									
,, 28									
Mar. 7	Leeds Med. 'A'	A							
,, 14	Old Roundheg's	H							
,, 21									
,, 28	Old Roundheg's	H							
April 4									
,, 11									
,, 18									
,, 25									

Others Pending.

Baildon's Fixtures for the 1941/42 season

Clubs increasingly had to rely on Services teams to fill gaps in their fixture lists as it now became clear that those clubs that had managed to play through the first two years of the war were unlikely to be joined by any more deciding to re-form. Life in Britain was very bleak. Many people in the towns and cities of Britain saw death and destruction at first hand. This was exemplified by an account from a Hymers School boy, Mike Read. Hymers School had been evacuated to Pocklington and on 18th September 1941 Mike was taking part in a rugby practice at Pocklington's Percy Road Ground when a Wellington Bomber crashed at nearby Northfield Farm. His account of the crash illustrates the reality of war in 1941. '*We heard a rising scream of a plane's engines and stopped playing to watch a Wellington roaring vertically downwards. A few seconds later the wings and tail parts tore off and fluttered off to follow the fuselage as it disappeared behind houses alongside the pitch to fall in a field at the far side of town.'* Sadly, the Wellington crash was a tragic accident in which eight aircrew lost their lives. That game of rugby must have lived with Mike Read for the rest of his life. The constant threat of the bombing raids had a massive impact on everyday life with the added anxiety, at this one of the lowest points in the war, of a possible German invasion of Britain. For the clubs currently playing, getting through the season and providing rugby for any players that wanted a game were their main priorities. Playing kit was now also becoming a big issue for some clubs. Clothes rationing that began on 1st June 1941 meant that it was very difficult for clubs to replace kit that was probably looking very shabby after at least two seasons of continuous use.

A Harrogate team pictured before a home fixture many of the players wearing different shirts.

The 1941/42 season was the last wartime season for some of the Yorkshire clubs that had been playing regular fixtures. The difficulty of raising a team was probably one of the major factors in the decision to close down. This was certainly the case with Brighouse Rangers who, although they were winning regularly, were really struggling to find fifteen players every week.

Brighouse Rangers Fixtures 1941/42

Sept	20th	Coll of Resurrection	Home
	27th	R.A.F. XV	Home
Oct	4th	Halifax	Away
	11th	Huddersfield O.B.	Home
	18th	Army XV	Away
	25th	Coll of Resurrection	Away
Nov	1st	Keighlians	Home
	8th	Army XV	Away
	15th	English Electric	Home
	22nd	Huddersfield O.B.	Away
	29th	Army XV	Home
Dec	6th	Keighlians	Away
	13th	Army XV	Home
	20th	Halifax	Home
	27th	Old Leodiensians	Away
Jan	3rd	Army XV	Home
	24th	Baildon	Away
Feb	14th	Baildon	Home
	21st	English Electric	Away
Mar	7th	R.A.F. XV	Home
	28th	Army XV	Away
April	4th	R.A.F. XV	Home
	11th	Old Leodiensians	Home

Over the previous season Brighouse had lost many of the men who played in the team that had reached the wartime cup final in 1940. One or two players had been replaced but the supply of newcomers was drying up as more as more young men joined the forces. Brighouse managed to struggle through the season but then obviously decided that it was too difficult to carry on. Headingley Old Boys and Baildon, two of the clubs that managed to play right through the war, had a number of near neighbours and were able to survive by offering a game to anyone from their area who wanted to play. In Leeds, Roundhay became a focus for rugby in the north of the city. The club welcomed newcomers, had a good ground and was also able to provide regular fixtures. A major issue for clubs to address in the 1941/42 season must have been the reduction in the call up age to eighteen that was announced by the Government in December 1941. To a large extent, many of the clubs still playing had relied on young players who had just left school but were not old enough to be called up into the Forces. From December 1941 on they were going to have to rely on men in reserved occupations and servicemen home on leave and looking for a game of rugby.

The majority of clubs that began the season managed to complete it, despite the very difficult times being endured both at home and abroad. The majority of Yorkshire's towns and cities continued to suffer from the German bombing. Hull, in particular, as is well documented, was under attack from 1940, and with large parts of the city destroyed by the high explosive and incendiary bombs that rained down on the city centre, the docks and industrial area. Goddard Avenue, where Hull and East Riding were based was bombed again in June 1941. Despite many parts of the city suffering terrible damage, with hundreds of people killed and injured, Hull and East Riding continued to organise fixtures. During these dark years of the war it will have been very difficult for rugby clubs to continue to operate, but amongst the people still organising fixtures there must have been a grim determination to carry on.

It is remarkable that rugby in Yorkshire managed to continue through this period. While some clubs closed down there was still plenty of rugby being played across the three Ridings. There is little doubt that despite the challenges there were clubs determined to continue. In Chapter

Two I mentioned the comments of J.M. Kilburn, in the Yorkshire Post On 21st October 1939, regarding the value of sport in difficult times. Life in 1942 was particularly difficult. Perhaps the people organising the Yorkshire rugby clubs had similar thoughts to those of Mr Kilburn as they overcame so many obstacles in order to provide a weekly game. Unfortunately, I have been unable to find any records of a sevens being organised in the West Riding in April 1942. However, despite the difficulties, Hull and East Riding did manage to organise their event. Travel issues and the small number of clubs now playing regularly could well have been the main reasons if, in fact, no sevens competitions took place in the West Riding.

However, towards the end of the 1941/1942 season there was one high point for rugby men in Yorkshire and that was a game organised by Bob Oakes between a Yorkshire Services XV and an RAF XV. The game took place on Saturday 14th March at Headingley, the home of Leeds Rugby League Club.

The RAF XV won by 19 points to 3 in front of a reasonable attendance who contributed £203 in gate receipts and a £43 collection for the RAF Benevolent Fund. In the Yorkshire team were three rugby league internationals, Stanley Brogden, Ken Jubb and Ted Tattersfield, and a Roundhay player James Dunlop. The RAF team had one rugby league international, Alan Edwards, who played for Dewsbury and Wales, and also a Northampton player, W. (Bill) Fallowfield. Bill Fallowfield played for England against Scotland in April 1942 and at the end of the war was appointed secretary of the Rugby Football League.

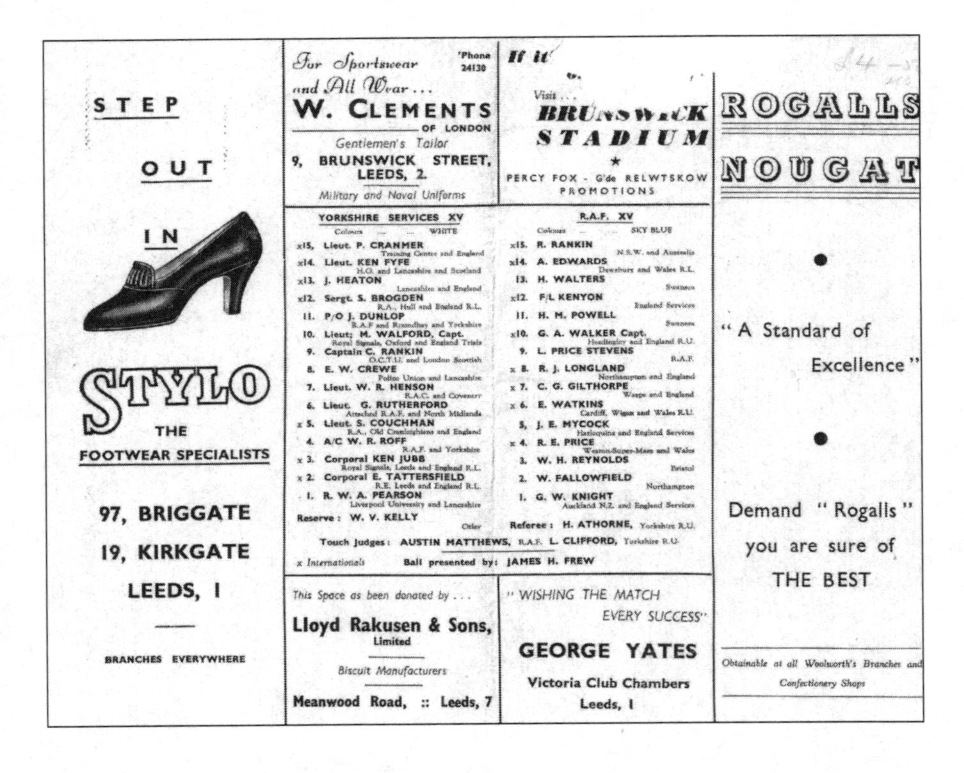

STEP

OUT

IN

STYLO

THE

FOOTWEAR SPECIALISTS

97, BRIGGATE

19, KIRKGATE

LEEDS, I

BRANCHES EVERYWHERE

For Sportswear and All Wear . . . 'Phone 24130

W. CLEMENTS OF LONDON

Gentlemen's Tailor

9, BRUNSWICK STREET, LEEDS, 2.

Military and Naval Uniforms

Visit . . .

BRUNSWICK STADIUM

★

PERCY FOX - G'de RELWTSKOW PROMOTIONS

YORKSHIRE SERVICES XV

Colours .... WHITE

x15, Lieut. P. CRANMER — Training Centre and England
x14. Lieut. KEN FYFE — H.Q. and Lancashire and Scotland
x13. J. HEATON — Lancashire and England
x12. Sergt. S. BROGDEN — R.A., Hull and England R.L.
11. P/O J. DUNLOP — R.A.F and Roundhay and Yorkshire
10. Lieut; M. WALFORD, Capt. — Royal Signals, Oxford and England Trials
9. Captain C. RANKIN — O.C.T.U. and London Scottish
8. E. W. CREWE — Police Union and Lancashire
7. Lieut. W. R. HENSON — R.A.C. and Coventry
6. Lieut. G. RUTHERFORD — Attached R.A.F. and North Midlands
x 5. Lieut. S. COUCHMAN — R.A., Old Cranleighians and England
4. A/C W. R. ROFF — R.A.F. and Yorkshire
x 3. Corporal KEN JUBB — Royal Signals, Leeds and England R.L.
x 2. Corporal E. TATTERSFIELD — R.E. Leeds and England R.L.
1. R. W. A. PEARSON — Liverpool University and Lancashire
Reserve : W. V. KELLY — Otley

R.A.F. XV

Colours .... SKY BLUE

x15. R. RANKIN — N.S.W. and Australia
x14. A. EDWARDS — Dewsbury and Wales R.L.
13. H. WALTERS — Swansea
x12. F/L KENYON — England Services
11. H. M. POWELL — Swansea
x10. G. A. WALKER Capt. — Headingley and England R.U.
9. L. PRICE STEVENS — R.A.F.
x 8. R. J. LONGLAND — Northampton and England
x 7. C. G. GILTHORPE — Wasps and England
x 6. E. WATKINS — Cardiff, Wigan and Wales R.U.
5, J. E. MYCOCK — Harlequins and England Services
x 4. R. E. PRICE — Weston-Super-Mare and Wales
3. W. H. REYNOLDS — Bristol
2. W. FALLOWFIELD — Northampton
1. G. W. KNIGHT — Auckland N.Z. and England Services

Referee : H. ATHORNE, Yorkshire R.U.

Touch Judges : AUSTIN MATTHEWS, R.A.F. L. CLIFFORD, Yorkshire R.U.

x Internationals — Ball presented by: JAMES H. FREW

This Space as been donated by . . .

Lloyd Rakusen & Sons, Limited

Biscuit Manufacturers

Meanwood Road, :: Leeds, 7

" WISHING THE MATCH EVERY SUCCESS"

GEORGE YATES

Victoria Club Chambers

Leeds, I

ROGALLS NOUGAT

• " A Standard of Excellence "

•

Demand " Rogalls " you are sure of THE BEST

Obtainable at all Woolworth's Branches and Confectionery Shops

What would the 1942/43 season bring?

Chapter Six

1942 – 1944

1942-43

For the majority of clubs, the 1942/43 season began on the 26th September 1942. The start to the season was made against a backdrop of further travel restrictions that hampered fulfilling fixtures for many still in action. A Government announcement at the end of July 1942 discouraged all but non-essential travel by car, and coach travel was also to be drastically reduced. This obviously meant that the main consideration when fixtures were organised was – could the opposition travel to the game? However, clubs were now used to overcoming the many challenges involved in continuing to play fixtures in such a time of adversity. I am sure that many players were suffering from the terrible bombing that continued across Yorkshire and from the anxiety for family and friends in the Services. The opportunity to play their chosen sport on a Saturday must have been very important in keeping up spirits during some of the darkest days of the war.

There was another increase in the number of games clubs were arranging against Services XVs, as in most cases these teams would have had access to transport. This meant that a fixture against a Services team was more likely to take place. Amongst the clubs back into action on the 26th September were Headingley Old Boys, Skipton, Keighlians, Huddersfield Old Boys and Roundhay. Old Leodiensians, who were playing their last season of wartime rugby, had actually started a week earlier on the 19th September with a fixture against Roundhay, probably organised because they were near neighbours.

Remarkably, two new names appeared on the Yorkshire rugby scene at the beginning of the 1942/43 season. Hunslet Engine Company was a team made up of employees of the large manufacturing company based in South Leeds. This team played a number of its home games in the 1942/43 season at Parkside, the home of Hunslet Rugby League Club. Hunslet Engine Company played regular fixtures during the season, beginning on the 3rd October 1942 with a game at Parkside against an R.A.S.C. XV. Hunslet Engine Company had a very competitive team and, as there was no other rugby union being played in the south of the city, they probably had the pick of the best available players.

The other new club was Wakefield Old Boys. During the 1942/43 season they played their home games at the King George Jubilee Playing Fields in Eastmoor, a suburb of Wakefield, before moving in 1943 to College Grove, the home of Wakefield RUFC. Wakefield Old Boys, originally formed by members of the County Hall Home Guard, was managed by Mr Doug Lloyd.

Another remarkable situation occurred in Hull where, despite the terrible death and destruction that the bombing caused, Hull and East Riding still managed to continue to play regular fixtures at its Goddard Road Ground. During this period clubs were often willing to move grounds in order to ensure a fixture took place. A good example was Headingley Old Boys, who played home games at their Hollin Lane Ground as well as moving across the city to play some home games at the Star and Garter Ground in Kirkstall.

Alongside the many Services teams that were playing regularly, a number of local Home Guard Units were also beginning to play fixtures. Wakefield County Hall Home Guard, mentioned above, was one example. Others were Heath Home Guard, in Halifax and Rotherham Home Guard. The Universities and Colleges were also playing regular fixtures and providing opposition for a number of clubs. The College of the Resurrection, a training college for priests, based in Mirfield, was playing regularly. The College had played fixtures before the war and continued to play during and after the war.

The number of representative matches also increased with one particularly interesting game taking place on 23rd January 1943 at Headingley, the home of Leeds Rugby League Club. This was a rugby union game organised by The Northern Command Sports Board between a Rugby League XV and a Rugby Union XV.

SOUVENIR PROGRAMME

NORTHERN COMMAND REPRESENTATIVE RUGBY MATCH

(Under the patronage of Lt. Gen. Sir T. R. EASTWOOD, K.C.B., D.S.O., M.C., G.O.C. in C. Northern Command)

UNION XV

VERSUS

LEAGUE XV

(Under Union Rules)

at

Leeds R.L. Football Club Ground

Headingley

(By kind permission of the Directors)

on

Saturday, January 23rd, 1943

Kick off 3-30 p.m.

ORGANISED BY THE NORTHERN COMMAND SPORTS BOARD.

The fixture attracted 8,000 spectators and raised £470 for the Army charities. The Rugby League XV won the game by 18 points to 11. It was reported that the rugby league forwards struggled to adapt to rugby union rules but their backs were too quick and skilful. When they were in possession their quick passing allowed them to dominate.

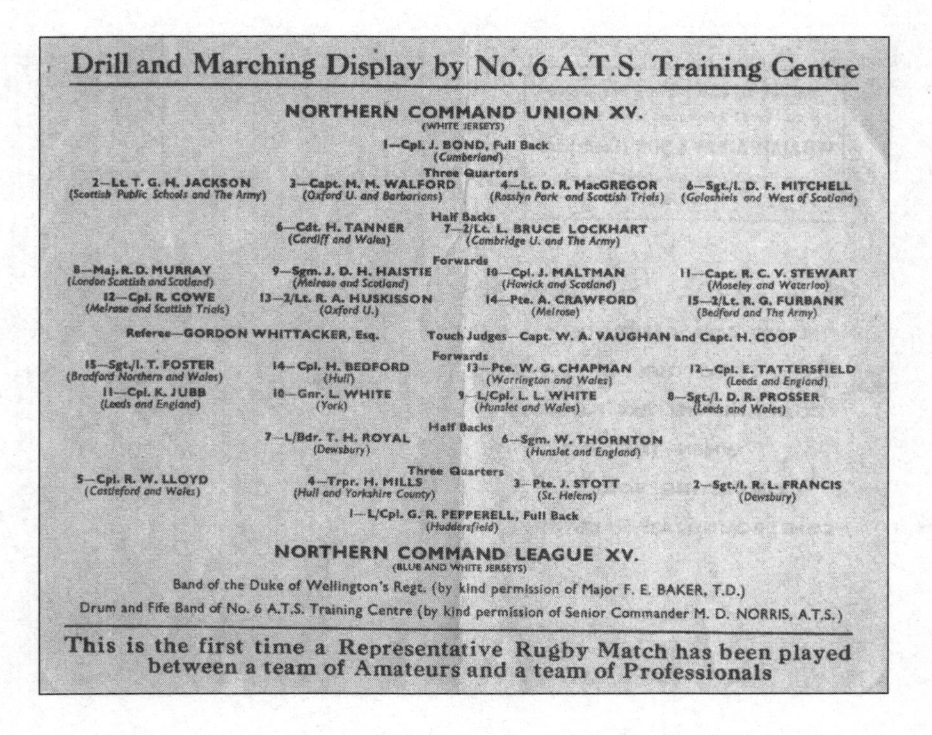

Drill and Marching Display by No. 6 A.T.S. Training Centre

NORTHERN COMMAND UNION XV.
(WHITE JERSEYS)

1—Cpl. J. BOND, Full Back (Cumberland)

Three Quarters

2—Lt. T. G. H. JACKSON (Scottish Public Schools and The Army)
3—Capt. M. M. WALFORD (Oxford U. and Barbarians)
4—Lt. D. R. MacGREGOR (Rosslyn Park and Scottish Trials)
6—Sgt./I. D. F. MITCHELL (Galashiels and West of Scotland)

Half Backs

6—Cdt. H. TANNER (Cardiff and Wales)
7—2/Lt. L. BRUCE LOCKHART (Cambridge U. and The Army)

Forwards

8—Maj. R. D. MURRAY (London Scottish and Scotland)
9—Sgm. J. D. H. HAISTIE (Melrose and Scotland)
10—Cpl. J. MALTMAN (Hawick and Scotland)
11—Capt. R. C. V. STEWART (Moseley and Waterloo)
12—Cpl. R. COWE (Melrose and Scottish Trials)
13—2/Lt. R. A. HUSKISSON (Oxford U.)
14—Pte. A. CRAWFORD (Melrose)
15—2/Lt. R. G. FURBANK (Bedford and The Army)

Referee—GORDON WHITTACKER, Esq. Touch Judges—Capt. W. A. VAUGHAN and Capt. H. COOP

Forwards

15—Sgt./I. T. FOSTER (Bradford Northern and Wales)
14—Cpl. H. BEDFORD (Hull)
13—Pte. W. G. CHAPMAN (Warrington and Wales)
12—Cpl. E. TATTERSFIELD (Leeds and England)
11—Cpl. K. JUBB (Leeds and England)
10—Gnr. L. WHITE (York)
9—L/Cpl. L. L. WHITE (Hunslet and Wales)
8—Sgt./I. D. R. PROSSER (Leeds and Wales)

Half Backs

7—L/Bdr. T. H. ROYAL (Dewsbury)
6—Sgm. W. THORNTON (Hunslet and England)

Three Quarters

5—Cpl. R. W. LLOYD (Castleford and Wales)
4—Trpr. H. MILLS (Hull and Yorkshire County)
3—Pte. J. STOTT (St. Helens)
2—Sgt./I. R. L. FRANCIS (Dewsbury)

1—L/Cpl. G. R. PEPPERELL, Full Back (Huddersfield)

NORTHERN COMMAND LEAGUE XV.
(BLUE AND WHITE JERSEYS)

Band of the Duke of Wellington's Regt. (by kind permission of Major F. E. BAKER, T.D.)

Drum and Fife Band of No. 6 A.T.S. Training Centre (by kind permission of Senior Commander M. D. NORRIS, A.T.S.)

This is the first time a Representative Rugby Match has been played between a team of Amateurs and a team of Professionals

The Northern Command Sports Board was very keen to organise other representative fixtures. However, when they attempted to organise a game against a Scottish Universities team, the Scottish RFU insisted that the Northern Command produce a signed declaration that no players would play for the Northern Command who had ever had connections with rugby league. The view of the Scottish RFU was not supported by the Yorkshire Secretary, Bob Oakes, who said that he believed that if a man was good enough to wear the King's uniform there should be no demarcation to stop him taking part in any game he wished. I can find no record of a Northern Command fixture with the Scottish Universities and so it seems unlikely that the Northern Command went ahead with the fixture as they were unwilling to exclude rugby league players from their teams.

Fixtures continued until the 26th April. One of the highlights of the season was the Northern Command Army Cup Final at Castleford Rugby League club's ground on 3rd April. The Yorkshire Army XV beat the Northumberland Army XV by 21 points to 5 in front of 3,000 spectators. On the 10th April, Headingley Old Boys played Hull and East Riding at their Hollin Lane ground. This was probably one of the few games played in Yorkshire that was not a local derby. On Saturday 17th April a sevens was held at Roundhay's Chandos Park Ground. Ten local teams took part including a number of Services sevens from the RAF and Army units. Roundhay School also fielded a team. Headingley Old Boys beat an ATC seven in the final of an event that raised money for the Red Cross Prisoners of War Fund. Headingley had recovered some of the player numbers from earlier in the season as, on the same afternoon, they were able to take fifteen players to Harrogate to play an RAF XV. The final Saturday of the season saw games with Roundhay, Hunslet Engine Company and Huddersfield Old Boys involved. While on the East Coast, Hull and East Riding held their annual sevens at their Goddard Avenue ground.

1943/44

In some respects the 1943/44 season was probably the most difficult for the clubs that had continued to play since September 1939, although the tide was turning in the war and the bombing of Yorkshire towns and cities was not as constant as it had been in 1941 and 1942. There were still air raids, particularly on Hull, and with the country bracing itself for the expected invasion of Europe, the focus for people in Britain must have been on winning the war as quickly as possible. The stalwarts who had kept rugby union going through the dark days in 1941 and 1942 could easily have decided to close down activities and wait for a victory over Germany that would signal a return to normality. However, most of the clubs did not choose this option and on the 11th September 1943 the new season began with a fixture between Baildon and Roundhay. Roundhay had managed, despite all the adversity, to play twenty six fixtures during the 1942/43 season.

Old Leodiensians had closed down at the end of the 1942/43 season but rugby continued to be played on their ground at Robin Hood, in South Leeds. Hunslet Engine Company took over the ground and played their home games there for the next two seasons. It also appears that 1942/43 was the last season that Keighlians played fixtures during wartime.

A representative fixture took place in Yorkshire on 16th October at Belle Vue, the home of Wakefield Trinity Rugby League Club. This game was between a Combined English and Welsh XV and a Scottish XV. It is clear from a statement on the programme cover that this game was being played under rugby union rules. There were no rugby league players selected by the Combined team, possibly at the insistence of the Scottish RFU. Perhaps the clarification on the programme was required by the Scottish RFU as they continued to be unwilling to allow any Scottish representative teams to play against Services teams that contained rugby league players. The game resulted in a fairly easy 41 points to 14 win for the Scottish XV but what the Scottish RFU thought about playing on a rugby league ground is not revealed. The reality in Yorkshire during the war years was that a majority of the rugby league grounds played host to rugby union teams. At club level games were played at places like Huddersfield, Hunslet, Keighley and York. Representative fixtures were often staged at Leeds, Bradford, Castleford and Wakefield. In Yorkshire there was a great deal of co-operation between the codes during the war years. Rugby league grounds were being maintained as there was a thriving professional rugby league competition during the war. The grounds also had good spectator facilities, and as the representative games were usually staged to raise funds for the wartime charities, it was sensible that grounds were used that would maximise the opportunity to raise funds. The value of representative fixtures as a contribution to the war effort was obviously reflected in the number of this type of fixture that was played. Also the income raised from the attendances at these games must have reflected the need for people to have a short distraction from the reality of life in wartime Britain. On 11th December, Castleford Rugby League Ground was used for a fixture between a West Riding Home Guard XV and a West Riding Army XV. Neither team boasted any really famous names but there were still 3,000 spectators at the game raising much needed funds for the British Red Cross and the local prisoners' fund.

Playing kit must have now been a massive issue after three years of clothes rationing. The RFU and the other British Unions approached the Board of Trade with a request for clothing coupon concessions similar to soccer. As a result of this approach, clubs were able to use spare coupons donated by supporters and members, but this supply must have been drying up as people needed to use all the coupons they were allocated to provide clothes for themselves and their families. West Hartlepool, a club based in the North East of England, came up with an unusual solution to the kit shortage. A supporter donated a number of flour bags that were then made into rugby shirts. The bags were pink and so the club bleached them, the result being fifteen white shirts. Whether clubs in Yorkshire followed this initiative is not known but, as the report about the flour bag shirts was published in the Yorkshire Post, it is possible that some enterprising officials considered doing the same.

A very significant representative fixture took place at Odsal Stadium on 29th April 1944 when a Rugby League XV met a Rugby Union XV in another game played under rugby union rules.

The League team won by 15 points to 10 mainly, it appears from contemporary reports, because of the speed and skill of their backs. Over13,000 spectators attended with more than £1,100 being taken in gate receipts. The Authorities had hoped for a bigger crowd and had obtained permission for up to 40,000 spectators to attend the game so 13,000 may have been disappointing. However, given the continuing travel problems the fact that over a £1,100 was raised for charity will have been some consolation.

COMBINED SERVICES RUGBY MATCH

(Organised by the Inter-Services Rugby Football Committee)

	RUGBY LEAGUE (All White, Blue and White Stockings)		RUGBY UNION (Red Jerseys, Blue Shorts, Red Stockings)	
15	L/Cpl. E. WARD, Army, Bradford N., England	Full Back	C.S.M.I. TROTT, Army, Penarth	15
14	Sgt.-Ins. R. L. FRANCIS, Army, Barrow, Wales	Right Wing Three-quarter	Lt. G. HOLLIS, R.N., Sale, England	14
13	Sgt. S. BROGDEN, Army, Hull, England	Right Centre Three-quarter	Capt. W. H. MUNRO, Army, Glasgow H.S.F.P., Scot.	13
12	Cfn. J. STOTT, Army, St. Helens, England	Left Centre Three-quarter	Lt. T. GRAY, Army, Heriots F.P., Scotland	12
11	Cpl. A. EDWARDS, R.A.F., Salford, Wales	Left Wing Three-quarter	Capt. J. R. S. INNES, Army, Aberdeen, G.S.F.P., Scot.	11
10	Sgt. W. T. H. DAVIES, R.A.F., Bradford N., Wales	Outside Half	Maj. C. R. BRUCE, Army, Glasgow Acads., Scotland	10
9	Bdr. H. ROYAL, Army, Dewsbury	Scrum Half	Lt. H. TANNER, Army, Swansea, Wales	9
8	Sgt.-Ins. D. R. PROSSER, Army, Leeds, Wales	Front Row Forward	Cpl. R. J. LONGLAND, R.A.F., Northampton, Eng.	8
7	L/Seaman C. J. CARTER, R.N., Leeds	Hooker Forward	Sgt. W. H. TRAVERS, Army, Newport, Wales	7
6	LAC. C. BRERETON, R.A.F., Halifax	Front Row Forward	Capt. R. E. PRESCOTT, Army, Harlequins, England	6
5	Sgt. D. MURPHY, Army, Bramley	Second Row Forward	Schoolmaster J. B. DOHERTY, R.N., Sale, England	5
4	F/Sgt. E. V. WATKINS, R.A.F., Wigan, Wales	Second Row Forward	Cpl. J. MYCOCK, R.A.F., Harlequins, England	4
3	Sgt. I. OWEN, R.A.F., Leeds, Wales	Back Row Forward	Capt. G. D. SHAW, Army, Gala, Scotland	3
2	Sgt. W. G. CHAPMAN, Army, Warrington, Wales	Back Row Forward	Capt. J. A. WATERS, Army, Selkirk, Scotland	2
1	Sgt.-Ins. T. FOSTER, Army, Bradford N., Wales	Back Row Forward	F/Lt. R. G. H. WEIGHILL, R.A.F., Waterloo, Eng.	1

Reserves:
LAC. J. LAWRENSON, R.A.F., Wigan, England
Lt. A. J. RISMAN, Army, Salford, Wales
L.A.C. S. PEPPERELL, R.A.F., Huddersfield, England
Sgt. J. RHODES, Army, Batley, N. Command

Captain: Sgt. W. T. H. DAVIES

Reserves:
Capt. W. C. W. MURDOCH, Army, Hillhead, H.S.F.P., Scotland
L/Cpl. J. KNOWLES, Army, Newport, Wales
Sgt. G. T. DANCER, R.A.F., Bedford, England
Capt. F. H. COUTTS, Army, Melrose, Scotland

Captain: Capt. R. E. PRESCOTT

Referee: Wing-Commander C. H. GADNEY, R.A.F.

Touch-judges: Capt. H. A. HAIGH-SMITH, Barbarians R.U.F.C.
Maj. E. L. THOMPSON, Northern Command, Harlequins

[All receipts at to-day's match are in aid of Services Charities]

Odsal had been used earlier in April when on the 15th a sevens organised by the Northern Command Sports Board was held. Again a Rugby League team was successful and an attendance of 5,000 raised £366 in gate receipts.

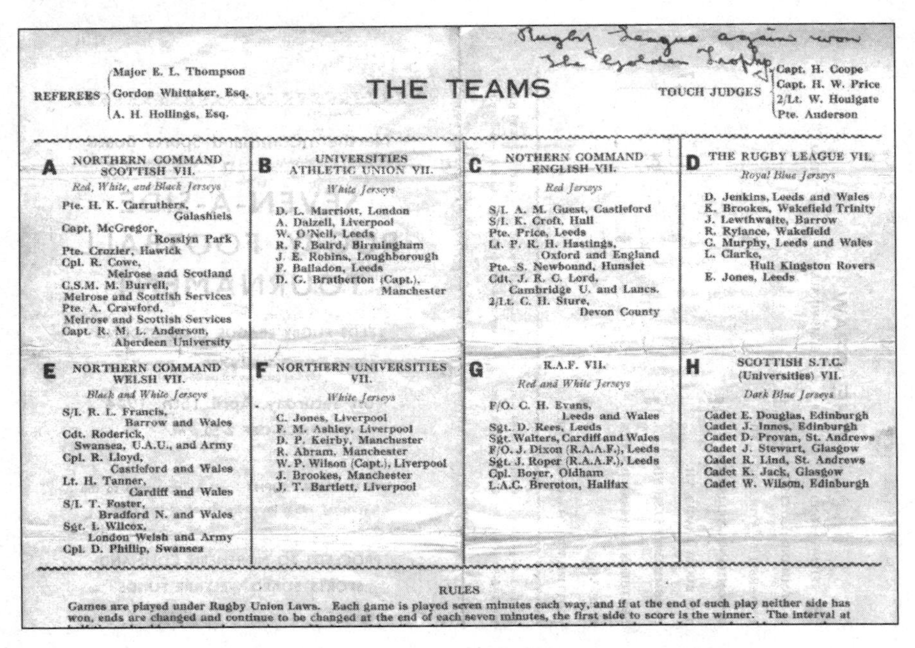

Rugby League again won the Golden Trophy

REFEREES: Major E. L. Thompson, Gordon Whittaker, Esq., A. H. Hollings, Esq.

THE TEAMS

TOUCH JUDGES: Capt. H. Coope, Capt. H. W. Price, 2/Lt. W. Houlgate, Pte. Anderson

A NORTHERN COMMAND SCOTTISH VII.
Red, White, and Black Jerseys
Pte. H. K. Carruthers, Galashiels
Capt. McGregor, Rosslyn Park
Pte. Crozier, Hawick
Cpl. R. Cowe, Melrose and Scotland
C.S.M. M. Burrell, Melrose and Scottish Services
Pte. A. Crawford, Melrose and Scottish Services
Capt. R. M. L. Anderson, Aberdeen University

B UNIVERSITIES ATHLETIC UNION VII.
White Jerseys
D. L. Marriott, London
A. Dalzell, Liverpool
W. O'Neil, Leeds
R. F. Baird, Birmingham
J. E. Robins, Loughborough
F. Balladon, Leeds
D. G. Bratherton (Capt.), Manchester

C NOTHERN COMMAND ENGLISH VII.
Red Jerseys
S/I. A. M. Guest, Castleford
S/I. K. Croft, Hull
Pte. Price, Leeds
Lt. P. R. H. Hastings, Oxford and England
Pte. S. Newbound, Hunslet
Cdt. J. R. C. Lord, Cambridge U. and Lancs.
2/Lt. C. H. Sture, Devon County

D THE RUGBY LEAGUE VII.
Royal Blue Jerseys
D. Jenkins, Leeds and Wales
K. Brookes, Wakefield Trinity
J. Lewthwaite, Barrow
R. Rylance, Wakefield
C. Murphy, Leeds and Wales
L. Clarke, Hull Kingston Rovers
E. Jones, Leeds

E NORTHERN COMMAND WELSH VII.
Black and White Jerseys
S/I. R. L. Francis, Barrow and Wales
Cdt. Roderick, Swansea, U.A.U., and Army
Cpl. R. Lloyd, Castleford and Wales
Lt. H. Tanner, Cardiff and Wales
S/I. T. Foster, Bradford N. and Wales
Sgt. I. Wilcox, London Welsh and Army
Cpl. D. Phillip, Swansea

F NORTHERN UNIVERSITIES VII.
White Jerseys
C. Jones, Liverpool
F. M. Ashley, Liverpool
D. P. Keirby, Manchester
R. Abram, Manchester
W. P. Wilson (Capt.), Liverpool
J. Brookes, Manchester
J. T. Bartlett, Liverpool

G R.A.F. VII.
Red and White Jerseys
F/O. C. H. Evans, Leeds and Wales
Sgt. D. Rees, Leeds
Sgt. Walters, Cardiff and Wales
F/O. J. Dixon (R.A.A.F.), Leeds
Sgt. J. Roper (R.A.A.F.), Leeds
Cpl. Boyer, Oldham
L.A.C. Brereton, Halifax

H SCOTTISH S.T.C. (Universities) VII.
Dark Blue Jerseys
Cadet E. Douglas, Edinburgh
Cadet J. Innes, Edinburgh
Cadet D. Provan, St. Andrews
Cadet J. Stewart, Glasgow
Cadet R. Lind, St. Andrews
Cadet K. Jack, Glasgow
Cadet W. Wilson, Edinburgh

RULES

Games are played under Rugby Union Laws. Each game is played seven minutes each way, and if at the end of such play neither side has won, ends are changed and continue to be changed at the end of each seven minutes, the first side to score is the winner. The interval at

Northern Comand Sevens

The Northern Command Sports Board continued to be very active in organising representative fixtures in Yorkshire. Earlier in the year they had managed to persuade a Scottish Services XV to play at the Leeds Rugby League Ground against a team containing a number of rugby league internationals. Perhaps the Scottish RFU did not have much influence over the activities of Services teams! The game on 15th March 1944 resulted in an easy victory for the Northern Command by 37 points to 5. Over 4,000 spectators saw rugby league players such as Ernest Ward, Gus Risman and Trevor Foster contribute to the victory.

Hull and East Riding held their annual sevens at Goddard Avenue, on Saturday 15th April. Headingley Old Boys made the long journey to the East coast to take part in the event. Roundhay also organised a sevens in 1944. The event took place on the 22nd April at Chandos Park, with the proceeds going to the Leeds General Infirmary. Alongside the usual Services teams were sevens from Baildon, Hunslet Engine Company and Headingley Old Boys.

Chapter Seven

1944 – 45

The sense of optimism in the country was reflected in what happened in Yorkshire rugby in 1944/45. Many people were convinced, particularly following the D Day landings in June 1944, that the end of the war was only months away. Clubs were still struggling with travel and kit issues but I am sure that the prevailing view in rugby circles what that 1944/45 would be the last wartime season.

For most clubs the season began on 23rd September 1944 with Huddersfield Old Boys again able to organise a full fixture list. For many there was still a heavy reliance on games with Services teams in order to ensure that they were able to play every week. For the two new clubs 1944/45 was to be their last season in existence. Hunslet Engine Company and Wakefield Old Boys had been very successful on the field but they only existed because of the war. Hunslet Engine Company was in full production throughout the hostilities. Because of that, many men working there were in reserved occupations and obviously valued the opportunity of a game of rugby as a short period of relaxation in a very hectic working week. Although these men were not soldiers on the front line, they still made a massive contribution to the war effort. Wakefield Old Boys had existed for different reasons. The club provided a focus for rugby union in its area of the West Riding. It gave an opportunity to play rugby to Service men on leave, as well as enjoyable entertainment for spectators at College Grove. Wakefield Old Boys was also able to take part in a number of fund raising fixtures with the money raised being donated to wartime charities.

After another full season of fixtures in 1943/44, Roundhay began their final wartime season on 16th September with a 20 points to nil victory over an RAFC XV. In 1943/44, Roundhay had played twenty nine games with fourteen victories. No doubt they were hoping to fulfil a similar number of fixtures and increase the number of victories. Amongst the clubs that began fixtures a week later than Roundhay were Headingley Old Boys, Huddersfield Old Boys and Hunslet Engine Company. Headingley Old Boys, who were now playing the majority of their home fixtures at Hollin Lane, had sufficient players available on the first Saturday of their season to field two teams. York, who had managed to play right through the war despite having no home ground, made a positive announcement in the Yorkshire Evening Press in September 1944 regarding their hopes for the new season. The intention at York was to improve their fixture list and attempt to organise games against most of the other club teams still in action. As the season got underway, Baildon, Skipton, Hull and East Riding and Wakefield Old Boys all got back into action.

Skipton's Fixtures for 1944/45 Season

Oct	7th	English Electric	Away
Nov	4th	Leeds Medicals	Away
	11th	R.A.P.C.	Home
	18th	Headingley O.B.	Home
	25th	Baildon	Home
Dec	2nd	Avro	Home
	16th	Headingley O.B.	Away
	30th	Baildon	Away
Jan	13th	Leeds Medicals	Home
	20th	R.A.P.C.	Away
Feb	3rd	English Electric	Home

Leeds Medicals and Leeds University provided fixtures for some of the Leeds area clubs and had been important, as had the Universities and Colleges in other parts of Yorkshire, in ensuring continuity of fixtures. Harrogate Old Boys announced an away fixture on 23rd September against Hunslet Engine Company and a return game against Hunslet, at Harrogate, on 14th October. It is not clear how many fixtures Harrogate played in the 1944/45 season but they were obviously preparing for a full return to action once peace was declared.

Some of the clubs in action in the 1944/45 season were widening their horizons and playing fixtures outside their local area. There were lots of local derbies on Huddersfield Old Boys fixture list but also games against Sale and York. In the pre and post war seasons a fixture against Sale would have been a big coup for Huddersfield. However, at a time when there was only a relatively small number of clubs in action, officials were happy to arrange fixtures with opponents that could be guaranteed to get fifteen players on the field, regardless of their perceived status. Sale also featured on York's fixture list for 1944/45, presumably because both clubs could travel by train to fulfil the fixture. York began their season on the 4th October with a game against an RAF XV that was played at Archbishop Holgate School. Hull and East Riding was also able to widen its horizons by travelling to Leeds in February 1945 for a fixture against Leeds Medicals.

One or two clubs seemed to be looking to the future and to an end of the hostilities by playing a few fixtures towards the end of the season. Halifax Vandals and Morley Grammar School Old Boys played in February and March. The clubs that had continued playing through the war years were obviously going to be better prepared for the start of the 1945/46 season than those that had closed down. Doubtless there were officials at the clubs that had not continued who would be busy in February and March preparing to put together their 1945/46 fixture lists.

The Northern Command continued to promote representative fixtures at the County's rugby league grounds. Headingley staging a fixture on 24th February against a Combined Universities XV that resulted in a 32 points to 6 victory to the Services team.

On the 28th April 1945 Roundhay staged its charity sevens at Chandos Park with teams from local clubs Baildon and Headingley Old Boys taking part. Hunslet Engine Company also entered a team in what may have been its last involvement with the rugby union scene in Yorkshire. Wakefield Old Boys, who did not take part in the Roundhay sevens, also ceased to play at the end of the 1944/45 season.

With the end of the war in Europe being declared on the 8th May 1945, the summer months would have seen many club officials working hard on their fixture lists, locating players and kit in readiness for the start of peacetime rugby in September 1945.

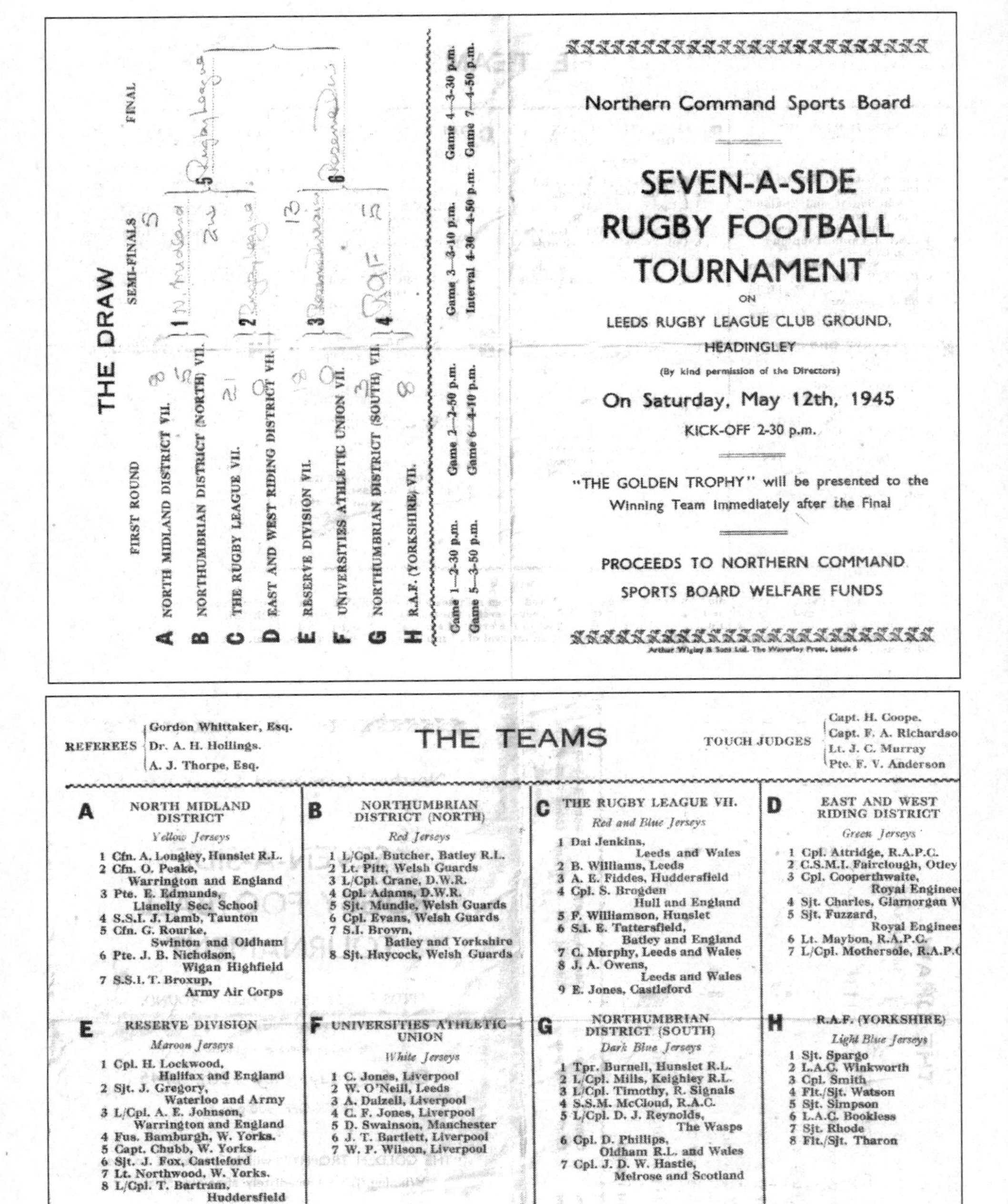

THE DRAW

FIRST ROUND

- A NORTH MIDLAND DISTRICT VII.
- B NORTHUMBRIAN DISTRICT (NORTH) VII.
- C THE RUGBY LEAGUE VII.
- D EAST AND WEST RIDING DISTRICT VII.
- E RESERVE DIVISION VII.
- F UNIVERSITIES ATHLETIC UNION VII.
- G NORTHUMBRIAN DISTRICT (SOUTH) VII.
- H R.A.F. (YORKSHIRE) VII.

SEMI-FINALS: 1, 2, 3, 4

FINAL: 5, 6

Game 1—2-30 p.m. Game 2—2-50 p.m. Game 3—3-10 p.m. Game 4—3-30 p.m.
Game 5—3-50 p.m. Game 6—4-10 p.m. Interval 4-30—4-50 p.m. Game 7—4-50 p.m.

Northern Command Sports Board

SEVEN-A-SIDE RUGBY FOOTBALL TOURNAMENT

ON

LEEDS RUGBY LEAGUE CLUB GROUND, HEADINGLEY

(By kind permission of the Directors)

On Saturday, May 12th, 1945

KICK-OFF 2-30 p.m.

"THE GOLDEN TROPHY" will be presented to the Winning Team immediately after the Final

PROCEEDS TO NORTHERN COMMAND SPORTS BOARD WELFARE FUNDS

Arthur Wigley & Sons Ltd. The Waverley Press, Leeds 6

THE TEAMS

REFEREES: Gordon Whittaker, Esq. / Dr. A. H. Hollings. / A. J. Thorpe, Esq.

TOUCH JUDGES: Capt. H. Coope. / Capt. F. A. Richardso / Lt. J. C. Murray / Pte. F. V. Anderson

A NORTH MIDLAND DISTRICT
Yellow Jerseys
1 Cfn. A. Longley, Hunslet R.L.
2 Cfn. O. Peake, Warrington and England
3 Pte. E. Edmunds, Llanelly Sec. School
4 S.S.I. J. Lamb, Taunton
5 Cfn. G. Rourke, Swinton and Oldham
6 Pte. J. B. Nicholson, Wigan Highfield
7 S.S.I. T. Broxup, Army Air Corps

B NORTHUMBRIAN DISTRICT (NORTH)
Red Jerseys
1 L/Cpl. Butcher, Batley R.L.
2 Lt. Pitt, Welsh Guards
3 L/Cpl. Crane, D.W.R.
4 Cpl. Adams, D.W.R.
5 Sjt. Mundle, Welsh Guards
6 Cpl. Evans, Welsh Guards
7 S.I. Brown, Batley and Yorkshire
8 Sjt. Haycock, Welsh Guards

C THE RUGBY LEAGUE VII.
Red and Blue Jerseys
1 Dai Jenkins, Leeds and Wales
2 B. Williams, Leeds
3 A. E. Fiddes, Huddersfield
4 Cpl. S. Brogden, Hull and England
5 F. Williamson, Hunslet
6 S.I. E. Tattersfield, Batley and England
7 C. Murphy, Leeds and Wales
8 J. A. Owens, Leeds and Wales
9 E. Jones, Castleford

D EAST AND WEST RIDING DISTRICT
Green Jerseys
1 Cpl. Attridge, R.A.P.C.
2 C.S.M.I. Fairclough, Otley
3 Cpl. Cooperthwaite, Royal Enginee
4 Sjt. Charles, Glamorgan W
5 Sjt. Fuzzard, Royal Enginee
6 Lt. Maybon, R.A.P.C.
7 L/Cpl. Mothersole, R.A.P.C

E RESERVE DIVISION
Maroon Jerseys
1 Cpl. H. Lockwood, Halifax and England
2 Sjt. J. Gregory, Waterloo and Army
3 L/Cpl. A. E. Johnson, Warrington and England
4 Fus. Bamburgh, W. Yorks.
5 Capt. Chubb, W. Yorks.
6 Sjt. J. Fox, Castleford
7 Lt. Northwood, W. Yorks.
8 L/Cpl. T. Bartram, Huddersfield

F UNIVERSITIES ATHLETIC UNION
White Jerseys
1 C. Jones, Liverpool
2 W. O'Neill, Leeds
3 A. Dalzell, Liverpool
4 C. F. Jones, Liverpool
5 D. Swainson, Manchester
6 J. T. Bartlett, Liverpool
7 W. P. Wilson, Liverpool

G NORTHUMBRIAN DISTRICT (SOUTH)
Dark Blue Jerseys
1 Tpr. Burnell, Hunslet R.L.
2 L/Cpl. Mills, Keighley R.L.
3 L/Cpl. Timothy, R. Signals
4 S.S.M. McCloud, R.A.C.
5 L/Cpl. D. J. Reynolds, The Wasps
6 Cpl. D. Phillips, Oldham R.L. and Wales
7 Cpl. J. D. W. Hastie, Melrose and Scotland

H R.A.F. (YORKSHIRE)
Light Blue Jerseys
1 Sjt. Spargo
2 L.A.C. Winkworth
3 Cpl. Smith
4 Flt./Sjt. Watson
5 Sjt. Simpson
6 L.A.C. Bookless
7 Sjt. Rhode
8 Flt./Sjt. Tharon

RULES

Games are played under Rugby Union Laws. Each game is played seven minutes each way, and if at the end of such play neither side has won, ends are changed and continue to be changed at the end of each seven minutes, the first side to score is the winner. The interval at half-time should not exceed one minute. No interval is allowed in the event of extra time being played. In case of accidents, no player may be replaced during the course of the game. There will be an interval of 20 minutes after the last semi-final. The final will consist of 10 minutes each way with a 3-minute interval.

The 1945 Northern Command Sevens

Chapter 8

1945-46

For most of the clubs still playing fixtures, the 1945/46 season began on 15th September 1945. However, Halifax and Keighlians were very quick off the mark and the first in Yorkshire back into action when they played each other on Saturday 1st September at Ovenden Park. Halifax won that game by 14 points to 5. They then played a return a week later at Keighley and in that game Keighley gained a narrow 10 points to 9 victory. Halifax had announced a full fixture list up to Easter 1945 and were obviously very keen to re-establish themselves as the strongest club in the Halifax District. Over the summer some of the clubs that had decided to close down during the war will have been holding meetings and making decisions regarding the feasibility of re-starting in September 1945. For many of those the decision was not straightforward, with the difficulty of finding suitable opponents one of the major considerations. Most clubs contemplating re-starting did not know whether they would have fifteen players available to begin the season, but more importantly the quality and experience of those players. The clubs like Roundhay, Huddersfield Old Boys and Baildon, were at an advantage as they had the nucleus of their first team and could continue to play opponents they had established relationships with during the war. The fixtures for those clubs in 1945/46 might not reflect their status pre-war but they knew that their opponents would be competitive. As the season progressed and more and more players returned, decisions regarding fixture lists in 1946 and beyond could be made with much more knowledge of playing strength. Those clubs that had members returning from the war were able to get back into action quickly. Some of the senior clubs, such as Headingley and Otley, were also able to play on the 15th September although in the case of Otley their team for the 1945/46 season was made up of players from both Otley and Ilkley. Ilkley had decided they did not have sufficient players available and would not consider re-starting in September 1945; a combined team was a logical short term solution. A selection of results from 15th September indicates that Yorkshire rugby had begun on the road to recovery.

Halifax 12 Headingley Old Boys 22
Harrogate Old Boys 9 Roundhay 6
Keighlians 24 English Electric 0
Otley 17 Baildon 3
Wakefield 45 RAF XV 5
Sandal 9 Scarborough 0
Waterloo 26 Headingley 6

Skipton 1st XV1945/46

As you can see from the results, victories like Headingley Old Boys at Halifax and Otley's close game at home to Baildon indicated that the strength of those clubs, in the early part of the new season, certainly did not mirror their strength in the 1930s. Huddersfield had organised a practice match for the 15th September and began their season the 22nd September, away to Headingley Old Boys. Bradford, Cleckheaton, and Sheffield were also soon back into action.

York, after their nomadic wartime existence, managed to arrange the use of York Railway Institute's New Lane ground for the 1945/46 season. York R.I. had decided that they would not attempt to re-start until 1946. The York club paid 7/6d a match to use the ground. The season began for York, on the 29th September, with an away game against Leeds Medical School. A young team was defeated by 24 points to 6, but despite the result officials were very optimistic for the future.

Pocklington was one of the clubs that certainly benefitted by managing to play through wartime. When a number of its players did return in 1945, its fortunes received an immediate boost. The men who returned were fitter and stronger and in some cases had gained much more rugby experience by playing for their unit and in Services representative teams. These men added to the agricultural workers who had been unable to join up as they were required to work on the land but had managed to continue to play some rugby. As a result Pocklington had an outstanding period of success in the immediate post-war years.

The Yorkshire RFU did not produce a handbook for the 1945/46 season. Instead a list of fixtures and contact details were distributed. The County decided that there would not be a Yorkshire Cup in the 1945/46 season. They also decided that the Yorkshire Wanderers would not play their usual Wednesday afternoon fixtures against the Public Schools. The collection of players from different parts of the County and the transport difficulties were cited as the main problems. The County did agree to play a number of representative fixtures but, would not be awarding caps for any of those games. A County trial was held at Headingley's Kirkstall ground on 13th October. This was obviously a necessity in this particular season as the County selectors were going to find it very difficult, after a six year break, to decide on which players were up to County standard. In the first County game of the season, Yorkshire played Lancashire on 20th October, at the Manchester Club's ground, losing by 26 points to 6.

Durham were Yorkshire's next opponents the following Saturday the 27th October. This fixture at Otley saw Yorkshire winning by 33 points to 8. On 24th November Cheshire provided the opposition, at Sale, the County again losing, and this time by 33 points to 8. The final Yorkshire fixture took place at Workington on 2nd March 1946 when Cumberland proved too strong winning by 27 points to 6. The Yorkshire officials were no doubt consoling themselves with the knowledge that many of the best players in the County had not yet returned from their wartime duties and that once they did results would improve.

LANCASHIRE COUNTY RUGBY FOOTBALL UNION.

Lancashire *v.* Yorkshire

at the Manchester R.U F.C., Moor Lane, Kersal.
Saturday, October 20, 1945. Kick-off 2-45 p.m.

Lancashire *(BLUE)*	**Yorkshire** *(WHITE)*
Full Backs	
16. Lt. M. T. Ackermann (England and South Africa)	15. S. A. F. Comer (Halifax)
Three Quarter Backs	
15. J. Walkley (Waterloo)	14. R. Pollard (Huddersfield Old Boys)
14. J. Heaton (*Capt.*) (Waterloo and England)	13. Alex. Gray (Sheffield)
12. Cpl. W. Gornall (Waterloo & England Reserve)	12. J. B. Womersley (Headingley)
11. C.S.M.I. C. B. Holmes (Manchester and England)	11. Lt. Gerry Hollis (*Capt.*) (Hull & E.R. & England)
Half Backs	
10. A. Openshaw (Fylde)	10. P/O. A. C. Towell (Middlesborough)
9. P. R. B. Jones (Waterloo)	9. Lt. W. J. Ellis (Headingley and England)
Forwards	
8. Maj. J. P. Dunkerley (Harlequins and England)	8. Drv. A. Cave (R.A.S.C.)
7. E. Evans (Sale)	7. L/Cpl. J. D. H. Hastie (Nrthn. Command & Scotl'd)
6. Dr. Logan (Waterloo)	6. G. H. Bottomley (Huddersfield Old Boys)
5. P. M. Rhodes (Manchester)	5. Pte. J. B. Lees (Nrthn Command & Scotl'd)
4. D. P. Sheedy (Sale)	4. P. Atkinson (Hull and E.R.)
3. H. F. Luya (Waterloo)	3. Ron. Peel (Headingley)
2. Cpl. J. Mycock (Sale and England)	2. Lt. Gordon Frank (Harrogate Old Boys)
1. E. P. Cosslett (Broughton Park)	1. L/Cpl. D. J. Reynolds (Northern Command)

Referee - P. D. COATMAN

November 3rd: LANCASHIRE v. CHESHIRE, at Waterloo
Nov. 10th: MANCHESTER v. BROUGHTON PARK, at Moor Lane

Programme 2d.

A surprising a number of the clubs that had closed down because of the war managed to re-start in September and October. However, several that had had their pitches ploughed up or clubhouses requisitioned were unable to play in 1945/46. Presumably the players from those clubs that wanted a game of rugby would have either had to wait until September 1946 or look for another club for the season. One club that did not play again after the war was Brighouse Rangers. After three very successful wartime seasons they had closed down due to the lack of players and, unfortunately, 1945 and peacetime did not improve the player situation.

The club had a very good ground and were so keen to continue that one of the remaining Brighouse officials approached Old Brodleians about relocating to Brighouse and playing under the Brighouse Rangers name. The offer was refused and rugby union was not played on the Lane Head ground again. The Old Brodleians club funds totalling £6 had been kept safe by a Mr Enright, the father of one of the players. He had kept the funds in his pocket right through the war. So with the princely sum of £6 in its funds, Old Brodleians was able to consider re-starting.

As the season got into full swing, Old Roundhegians and Morley announced that they would be playing fixtures. Morley decided to hold a meeting on 8th October in order to gauge the support they had for re-starting. The club was aware that there would be very few players available who had played pre-war and that they were going to have to rely on a very young team in order to fulfil their fixtures. Morley were back in action in October with an away game at Baildon. Old Roundhegians also began fixtures in October with a game against Roundhay 'A'. On the 20th October Huddersfield Old Boys had one of their best results of the season when they beat Headingley by 18 points to 11 at Kirkstall. Their victory was inspired by Haydn Tanner, the Welsh international scrum half, who was still in the Army and stationed at Catterick Camp in the North Riding. Presumably, someone Haydn Tanner knew from Huddersfield Old Boys invited him to play for them. The following week Tanner was named in the Yorkshire County team to play Durham. However, he did not take part in this fixture as he was asked to captain his club Swansea in a fixture against a New Zealand Army XV.

Confirmation that the balance of power in the county had definitely shifted in this first peacetime season came from J.M. Kilburn, the Yorkshire Post's rugby union correspondent, who noted on 1st November that, '*Some of the match results today would have seemed incredible pre-war, evidence of the changed and changing circumstances of many clubs.'* Mr Kilburn singled out Keighlians and Headingley Old Boys for particular praise, suggesting that the style of rugby played by those two had been a key to their success in the early months of the season.

In the East of the County Hull and East Riding and Old Hymerians were soon playing again. A joint trial game between the two was held on 22nd September 1945 at the Old Hymerians Ground with a good attendance of players from both clubs. Two weeks later both had fixtures organised. On 6th October at Goddard Avenue Hull and East Riding entertained Headingley. The Leeds club, who arrived with only fourteen players, was loaned a man and then went on to win by 9 points to 5. For both the Hull clubs a full fixture list was organised for the 1945/46 season with many familiar opponents and fixtures in the West Riding featuring again.

Bradford had been dominant in the first year of wartime rugby but, because in 1940 it had lost many of its leading players the club, had decided to close down. In September 1945 Bradford was beginning to build up its playing strength and working to overcome vandalism problems at its Lidget Green Ground. The club had held a meeting in the summer of 1945 with a view to deciding how to deal with damage that the vandals had caused during the war. The ground, that had hosted County games pre-war, was in a terrible state but fortunately, through the efforts of the committee, most of the repairs were undertaken and by early January the facilities were able to sustain regular rugby. The club had fielded two teams since re-starting and the first team managed to win nine of the fifteen games played before Christmas. Bradford was expecting to run three teams in the 1946/47 season with a number of their old opponents returning to the fixture list.

By the turn of the year, all the clubs that were going play in the 1945/46 season had been in action and a number that had not re-started were making plans to begin fixtures again in September 1946. In February, Keighlians beat Wakefield to end that clubs thirty one game winning sequence. A Yorkshire County meeting held in February heard stories from places like Barnsley and Upper Wharfedale where officials were planning for the next season. In other parts of the County clubs were organising fixture lists and letting former players returning from the Services know that they would be back in action.

In April and early May, seven a side competitions took place at Hull and East Riding, Skipton, Roundhay and Huddersfield. These competitions were mostly dominated by the senior clubs, with Hull and East Riding beating Headingley to win their sevens on 13th April. Roundhay won the Skipton sevens, held on Easter Monday the 22nd April.

While in the Roundhay seven a side competition held on 27th April Bradford beat Wakefield in the final. In the Huddersfield Old Boys sevens on 4th May the home club beat Broughton Park in the final. Perhaps Huddersfield had benefitted from keeping a 1st XV together through the war years. In the fifteen a side game Huddersfield had a good season picking up victories against Sale, Roundhay and Otley, as well as the Haydn Tanner inspired victory over Headingley.

Huddersfield Old Boys 1st XV 1945-46

Roundhay played thirty games in 1945/46, winning sixteen of them. Unfortunately, I have been unable to locate any other club records for the 1945/46. It would have been interesting to compare the records of some clubs in the first peacetime season with those in the last season before the war. My assumption is that for many rugby people in

Yorkshire seeing, a number of clubs playing regularly was probably the most important aspect of the 1945/46 season.

I am sure that many rugby people in Yorkshire were surprised at how well the game recovered after the war. Although standards were not as high as in the pre-war years, clubs had fulfilled weekly fixtures, repaired their grounds after in some cases six years of neglect, and built up their playing strength. The County handbook for 1946/47 indicates that, for many, one team was all they could organise. 1945/46 must have been even more difficult, and it is a tribute to their administrators that clubs were able to fulfil weekly fixtures. At the Annual General Meeting of the County on 24th June 1946, Bob Oakes, the long serving County Secretary, gave a very optimistic report that was echoed at the same meeting by Mr H.J. White, the Yorkshire County President. Both men expected that Yorkshire rugby would continue to build in skill and capacity, and that the clubs and County team would soon return to full strength again.

Chapter Nine

The Survivors

An intriguing question that presents itself is why was there more rugby played in the West Riding during the war years than in any other part of Yorkshire?

In the 1930s the strongest Yorkshire clubs were in the cities and towns of this part of Yorkshire. However, I doubt whether those that did continue would have been predicted in 1939. Roundhay and Huddersfield Old Boys had both been reasonably successful pre-war. They had their own grounds, good facilities and a large membership. In the 1938/39 season, both had organised fixtures for three teams on Saturday's and, in Huddersfield's case one additional team on a Wednesday afternoon. However, there were many other West Riding clubs in a similar and in some cases better position, having a much bigger playing membership. Was it the loss of key playing personnel, or was it the loss of important officials, that led to some closing down? All the clubs that continued to play right through the war appeared to accept that the game was more important than the result. An opportunity to get away from the horrors of war for one afternoon a week either as players or spectators must have been important in maintaining morale, just as was the continuation of cinema, theatre and professional sport. The sense of normality that came with regular fixtures at their local rugby ground must have been a big motivating factor for the people who continued to organise club rugby union.

Huddersfield Old Boys were, in many respects, one of the most successful and best organised West Riding clubs between 1939 and 1945.

Huddersfield had produced emergency fixture cards every season, collated results, held meetings and in many ways continued as normal.

Huddersfield Emergency Fixture Card

Roundhay were similar in that results were collated, full fixture lists organised and a seven a side event took place at their Chandos Park ground even in some of the darkest years of the war. Baildon was an unusual survivor. Their facilities did not match those of Roundhay and Huddersfield and the club had only organised two teams pre-war. Baildon also had competition from a very strong Bradford club as well as near neighbours Bingley and Keighlians. The assumption must be that the officials at Baildon welcomed any young men from their part of the Riding who wished to play rugby and also must have actively recruited players throughout the war. Skipton, another of the survivors, possibly benefitted from having a much larger catchment area for players. Also, as it was in a rural part of the West Riding, Skipton did not suffer from the severe bombing that places like Leeds, Hull and Sheffield had to endure.

The clubs

The majority of the clubs that survived were based in the West Riding. The notable exceptions were Hull and East Riding from the East Riding of Yorkshire and York, based in the city that was not considered, in local government terms to be part of any of the three Ridings. In my view, the answer to the question I posed at the beginning of this chapter must be that where there are major centres of population there are likely to be more potential opponents within a reasonable travelling distance, even in wartime. Although Hull and East Riding was not in the West Riding, the club's survival could be because it was based in Hull, the largest centre of population in the East Riding. An exception to this theory is the survival of Skipton. However, it is possible that Skipton survived because of the proximity of a number of Service units, which provided many of the club's opponents in the later years of the war.

I am going to begin this section of the chapter with Huddersfield Old Boys who not only kept going through the war but also kept detailed records, many of which survive today.

Huddersfield Old Boys

The Huddersfield Old Boys reacted very quickly once it was clear, in September 1939, that clubs were able to organise fixtures and continue to operate if they felt they had sufficient players. After the stuttering start seen at all the Yorkshire clubs that re-started in September, Huddersfield organised fixtures every Saturday. A number of players had been called up but Huddersfield overcame that problem in the early months of the 1939/40 season. Officials were obviously mindful of the need to continue to recruit any players that had not been called up and might still be available. Walter Scott, the Honorary Secretary, issued a rallying call on the 11th November 1939, headed '*H.O.B. v Hitler & Co.*' The appeal was for players to inform him of their availability in order that Huddersfield Old Boys could survive.

The letter produced a good response and the club was able to continue to organise and fulfil fixtures every week.

On 23rd September Huddersfield began their wartime campaign with a fixture against 214 Battery of the Royal Artillery. Fixtures were then organised mainly against local opposition, such as the Huddersfield YMCA, who managed to play a few games in the 1939/40 season. The College of the Resurrection in Mirfield also provided opposition, as did some of the Halifax District clubs that had begun to play regular fixtures again. There was a determination amongst the members that,

HUDDERSFIELD OLD BOY'S
Rugby Football Club.

President: H. S. NETHERWOOD, Esq.

Longwood House,
Fixby,
Huddersfield.
Nov. 11th, 1939.

H. O. B. v. HITLER & CO.

Dear Sir,

This is an appeal for you to play your part in a very strenuous contest and we trust you will respond generously.

The call to arms at the commencement of the season met with a ready response from our playing members and officials, and up to date over a hundred members including our President are with the Forces, or engaged in National Service.

Our ground has been placed at the disposal of the members of His Majesty's Forces and as occasion arises one team is being turned out to play local sides so long as players are available.

A great responsibility devolves upon those still at home if the club is to be kept in existence and ready to carry on its good work when hostilities cease.

Our pavilion is already closed and the furniture stored perchance the building is required for National Service. Certain expenses still go on and funds will be required to keep the ground, stand and buildings in good order.

The Rugby Football Union have given a fine lead and have excused our ground payments for the war period. The Kirkburton Urban District Council have very generously excused a large portion of our rates. We now appeal to all our members to continue payment of their subscriptions and to send along this year's contribution as early as possible.

When the lads return to civil life, one of the greatest pleasures will be to don the old colours and play the game they love so well.

It is our duty to keep the flag flying and I trust we may rely on your early co-operation and continued support.

Do please send along your subscription either to me or to either of our Treasurers.

Yours faithfully,
WALTER A. SCOTT,
Hon. Sec.

H.O.B. v Hitler & Co

regardless of how difficult things became, Huddersfield Old Boys would continue to play regular fixtures. The facilities at Waterloo, their home ground, were also in demand as early as the 9th September 1939, when the pavilion was taken over for use as a decontamination unit. Later in the war, plans were made by Kirkburton Council to turn part of the pavilion into a British Restaurant.

This was a Government initiative to provide communal kitchens to ensure local communities and people who had run out of rationing coupons were still able to eat. The plans for a British Restaurant were opposed by the club committee, as they did not believe they were feasible. Huddersfield Old Boys had already given permission for part of the pavilion to be used as an emergency feeding centre in the event of a blitz and for use as a centre for the Council's warships collection. As there was already a decontamination unit in the pavilion,

KIRKBURTON URBAN DISTRICT COUNCIL.

23 JOHN WILLIAM STREET,

HUDDERSFIELD.

G. W. SMITH, F.C.A.
G. G. SMITH, A.C.A., M.A.
JOINT CLERK
AND
CHIEF FINANCIAL OFFICER.

PHONE { KIRKBURTON 216-217.
HUDDERSFIELD 3788-3789.

6th. June, 1942.

Walter A.Scott, Esq.,
Longwood House,
Fixby, Huddersfield.

Dear Sir,

HUDDERSFIELD OLD BOYS' RUGBY FOOTBALL CLUB

I duly received your letter of the 1st. June, and the matter has been mentioned to Mr. Clifford. We are waiting to hear from the Ministry of Health as to whether they agree to a proposed scheme, and upon hearing from them would have communicated with you.

If the Scheme is agreed the Council would approach your Club to take the Pavilion on terms to be agreed with the District Valuer.

Yours faithfully,

Joint-Clerk.

Letter from Kirkburton Council

the committee could not see how the Council's restaurant plan would work. There were meetings held and letters written and although plans became quite advanced, the British Restaurant was never opened.

As well as continuing to play regular fixtures right through the war years, the club also held schoolboy matches at Waterloo and fund raising fixtures for the Services charities. They also gave permission for Services teams to use the ground. Huddersfield Old Boys assisted the war effort in 1940 by allowing a local farmer to graze his animals on the 'B' team pitch. In 1943 the same farmer was allowed to plough up the 'B' team pitch in order to plant crops. Despite losing one hundred and fifty players to the forces, there were always sufficient players available every Saturday in order to continue to fulfil fixtures. The hard working committee continued to meet regularly and keep detailed records of their meetings and of the fixtures played and the players taking part in them. Those records provide a picture of just how committed the club members were to ensure that rugby continued in Huddersfield, and in H.O.B. v Hitler and Co. H.O.B. were the winners.

Roundhay

Roundhay, no longer in existence following its merger with Headingley in 1992, kept the flag flying in North Leeds. The club lost many players in the early years of the war. Despite losing more games than it won in four of the six wartime seasons, Roundhay still managed to provide regular fixtures every year. The club also raised funds for local charities by organising its annual sevens. Unfortunately, because Roundhay's minute books and records of wartime activity are no longer in existence; it is not clear whether the sevens happened in every one of the six seasons. Fortunately, however, there is still a record in existence of the number of fixtures played and the wins, losses and draws in all the wartime seasons.

1939/40	*P 38*	*W 13*	*L23*	*D2*
1940/41	*P21*	*W11*	*L7*	*D3*
1941/42	*P24*	*W10*	*L11*	*D3*
1942/43	*P26*	*W12*	*L14*	*D0*
1943/44	*P29*	*W14*	*L15*	*D0*
1944/45	*P25*	*W18*	*L6*	*D1*

Baildon

Baildon is a club currently operating in Yorkshire Three. During the war, it was a focus for rugby activity in Bradford which meant that it was able to arrange fixtures against opponents that would be considered much higher in the 'pecking order'. In the early years of the war the club had fixtures with Otley, Roundhay, Bradford and Halifax, all clubs that would not have normally contemplated fixtures with Baildon. One of the reasons for the club surviving was that the officials were able to continue their involvement in rugby right through the war. Mr J.S. Armstrong was the General Secretary during all the wartime seasons, with Mr H. Kitson Junior, Mr E. Midgley, Mr J. Trenholme, Mr A.E. Gillard, Mr A. Mc Farlane and Mr J. Bell, the stalwarts who all held official positions at an obviously very well run organisation. The club produced a fixture card every year and was able to organise a full fixture list prior to the start of each season. Baildon held regular meetings and took great pride in fulfilling its fixtures despite the difficulties. As was the case at most of the surviving clubs, results were far less important than playing regular fixtures. As you can see from the list below, Baildon won very few games in the later war years, but that certainly did not dampen the enthusiasm of the officials.

1939/40	*P 21*	*W 10*	*L 11*
1941/42	*P 13*	*W 3*	*L 8*
1942/43	*P 29*	*W 7*	*L 22*
1943/44	*P 21*	*W 4*	*L 17*
1944/45	*P 23*	*W 7*	*L 15*

Unfortunately, the list does not include information from the 1940/41 season. The club did have a full fixture list for that season but the results were not recorded in the minutes of the 1941 Annual General Meeting.

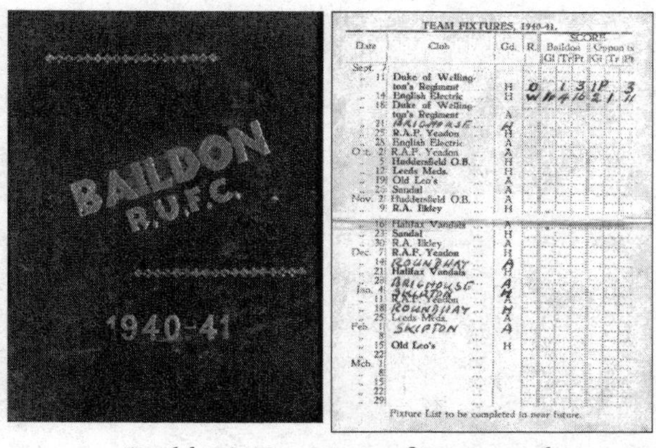

TEAM FIXTURES, 1940-41.

Date		Club	Gd.	R.	Baildon Gl	Baildon Tr	Baildon Pt	Opponents Gl	Opponents Tr	Opponents Pt
Sept.	7									
"	11	Duke of Wellington's Regiment	H	D		1	3	1P		3
"	14	English Electric	H	W	1	4	16	2	1	11
"	18	Duke of Wellington's Regiment	A							
"	21	BRIGHOUSE	H							
"	25	R.A.F. Yeadon	H							
"	28	English Electric	A							
Oct.	2	R.A.F. Yeadon	A							
"	5	Huddersfield O.B.	H							
"	12	Leeds Meds.	H							
"	19	Old Leo's	A							
"	26	Sandal	A							
Nov.	2	Huddersfield O.B.	A							
"	9	R.A. Ilkley	H							
"	16	Halifax Vandals	A							
"	23	Sandal	H							
"	30	R.A. Ilkley	A							
Dec.	7	R.A.F. Yeadon	H							
"	14	ROUNDHAY	A							
"	21	Halifax Vandals	H							
"	28	BRIGHOUSE	A							
Jan.	4	SKIPTON	H							
"	11	R.A.F. Yeadon	A							
"	18	ROUNDHAY	H							
"	25	Leeds Meds.	A							
Feb.	1	SKIPTON	A							
"	8									
"	15	Old Leo's	H							
"	22									
Mch.	1									
"	8									
"	15									
"	22									
"	29									

Fixture List to be completed in near future.

Baildon's Emergency fixture card

During the wartime seasons, Baildon responded to many challenges both on and off the field. Fundraising was a major issue for many of the clubs that survived. At Baildon, the lack of social events in the early years of the war meant that after the profit made in 1939/40 season the Treasurer often reported a small loss. The committee looked at a number of ways of generating income with one of the most successful taking place on 23rd September 1944 at the Victoria Hall, Saltaire. A dance was held there, attracting five hundred and twenty two people and generating a profit of £30 8s 7d. Remarkably one hundred and fifty five Forces personnel attended the dance, an indication of how important the involvement of local Services units was to the survival of club rugby.

Headingley Old Boys

Unfortunately Headingley Old Boys is no longer in existence as, following the loss of its ground, it merged with Leeds Chirons in 1956. However, despite going out of existence only ten years after the war, the wartime years and the 1945/46 season could be seen as some of the most successful in the club's history. Headingley attracted many experienced players during the war years, including a number of County players who made a big contribution to the club's success. I documented in Chapter Two how Headingley Old Boys re-organised its activities in November 1939 and from that point on organised fixtures in all the six wartime seasons, often having sufficient players for two teams. The club built on its wartime success in 1945/46, when it could have been considered one of the strongest in Yorkshire. It is interesting to speculate that if there had been a Yorkshire Cup held in 1945/46, then perhaps Headingley Old Boys would have been considered one of the favourites. Headingley Old Boys managed to play through the war despite using a number of different grounds, a handicap that the club seemed to overcome with ease. Most of the fixtures had been played at Hollin Lane, in the Headingley area of Leeds, but the club used other grounds in North and West Leeds and also Becket Park, where Leeds Training College was based.

Hull and East Riding

Throughout the war Hull and East Riding managed to continue to play home games and an annual seven a side competition at their Goddard Avenue ground. The ground was in a part of Hull that did suffer badly from the bombing raids that the city endured from 1940 until 1945. Despite the terrible devastation wreaked by the German bombers the club still continued to organise and play fixtures there. As I mention earlier, Hull and East Riding was able to supplement club fixtures with games against Services teams, schools and the University College. In September 1939 the club made an appeal in the Hull Daily Mail for players to contact officials if they were able to play. The appeal resulted in sufficient players being available for the first fixture on 14th October 1939. In the first season of the war, other local clubs such as Old Hymerians, Hessle and Hull Brunswick were all playing as were Driffield and Goole Grammar School Old Boys from slightly farther a-field. By the middle of November sufficient players were available for Hull and East Riding to be able to organise an 'A' team. The 'A' team was a luxury that did not occur every week and, as the war continued, fielding two teams became a rare event. The club was able to organise its first wartime sevens in April 1940 and the tradition continued right through the war, the money raised being donated to a variety of local wartime charities. By the end of 1941, Hull and East Riding was the only club still operating in Hull. The fixtures organised from 1941 onwards were mainly against Services teams, the Hull University College and, in the later years of the war, Headingley Old Boys and Leeds Medicals. The fixtures against Headingley Old Boys and Leeds Medicals were made possible by the good rail links between the two cities. For their fixture against Headingley Old Boys on 28th October, 1944, the Hull players were told to meet at Hull Railway Station in order to travel on the 12.25 pm train to Leeds. Headingley was the only club to feature regularly in the Hull and East Riding fixtures and also take part in the annual sevens. Once the other Hull clubs closed down, the teams taking part in the sevens were mainly drawn from the Services, the National Fire Service and Hymers School.

Players taking part in the Hull and East Riding Sevens in 1943

Hull and East Riding dominated the seven a side competitions, winning the 1942, 1943 and 1944 events. In 1945, Headingley Old Boys brought a very strong team to the event and won the final.

Pocklington

Pocklington was very active during the war but did not play as many fixtures as some of the other clubs that survived. During the six wartime seasons Pocklington played a total of twenty six games, with fourteen victories, eleven defeats and one draw. However, eleven of the twenty six games took place in 1939/40 season. In the seasons that followed, Pocklington kept the flag flying by playing a few fixtures each season and also promoting an annual Easter game at their Percy Road ground between two local schools.

It can be said that at Pocklington one man kept the club functioning during the war. Eric Scaife, who was the Estate Manager at Warter Priory, took control acting as Captain, Secretary and Treasurer. Mr Scaife had help from a small number of the remaining pre-war players and established strong links with the Services units based in the area and also the local schools. The Army, RAF bases and schools provided the opposition for most of Pocklington's wartime fixtures. There were

The Pocklington Schools Cup Winners

thirty nine Pocklington players who served their country in World War Two and this meant that, as well as providing opposition, the Army, RAF and schools also provided players for the club. It appears that the relaxation of the RFUs professionalism rules allowed Pocklington to regularly include rugby league players in their fixtures. Many of these players were no doubt stationed at RAF Pocklington where Squadron Leader Gus Walker, a former England rugby union stand-off, was able to ensure that many of the best rugby players in the RAF flew back to Pocklington for games. William Cobby, an England player in 1900, also turned out for Pocklington on occasions. It is remarkable that a club as far from the main population centres as Pocklington was able to survive. However, it is clear that where clubs did survive in the less populated parts of the county the crucial factors were at least one enthusiastic organiser and good links with the local Service units. Pocklington had both.

Selby

The fact that Selby managed to play right through the war was mainly because of the enthusiasm and commitment of two club officials. The brothers Don and Walter Jackson kept Selby going, arranging a full fixture list every season. Selby was situated close to a number of Services units and, by organising fixtures with these units and also encouraging Servicemen to play for the club, the Jacksons ensured that Selby was playing regularly. In the first two years of wartime rugby Selby was playing both against locally based Services teams but also against York, York Railway Institute, Roundhay and Morley. Selby's opportunity to play against clubs in Leeds must have decreased as the wartime travel restrictions began to have an impact, although Leeds Medics and Leeds University did continue to feature on the fixture list. The good rail links between York and Selby meant that they played against each other a number of times each season. Towards the end of the war, York was the only club team to appear regularly on Selby's fixture list. The reports on Selby's wartime activities gradually disappear from the local newspapers from 1943 onwards,

Selby R.U.F.C. - Season 1943-44

Month	Day	Opponent	Venue	Result	Score
Oct	2	R.A.F. Sherburn..	.A	W	15-9
	16	Leeds University ..	.A	W	19-5
	30	N0.2P.T.C.............	.H	L	6-14
Nov.	6	R.A.F. Sherburn..	.H	W	9-8
	20	R.E'sSnaith	..	L	3-13
	27	York	..A	W	8-0
Dec.	11	York	..		Cane.
	27	Household Cav....	..	W	10-9
Jan.	1	Reccon. Corp	..	L	8-24
	8	N0.2P.T.C.............	..A	L	0-8
	15	Leeds Univ	..		Cane.
	22	AVRO Yeadon	..	W	16-3
	29	Reccon. Corp	..A		Cane.
Feb.	5	AVRO Yeadon	..A	L	3-11
	12	R.E's Goole	..	W	16-6
	19	Hull A.T.C.............	..A	W	5-0
	26	R.A.F. Holme-on- Spalding Moor.	.. H	D	10-10
Mar.	4	York	..	L	13-17
	11	Leeds Medics........	..A		Cane.
	18	York	..A	L	3-15
	25	R.A.F. Holme-on- Spalding Moor.	..	D	6-6
April	1	Leeds Medics........	..	L	3-8
	8	York	..	W	22-3
	10	E.M. Household Cavalry..................	..	W	11-3
	15	R.A.F. Holme-on- Spalding Moor.	..A	L	3-17

P 21, W 10, D 2, L 9, For 189, Against 189.

Season 1944/5

P 24, W 14, D 1, L 9, For 182, Against 150.

Wartime Results

Selby's Fixtures and results for the 1943-44 season

but fortunately, as you can see from the illustration, Don and Walter Jackson kept detailed records of the club's wartime fixtures. These records indicate that Selby was very competitive during the war and when a game was lost it was often only by a few points.

Skipton

I have included Skipton in the group of clubs that managed to play right through the war because contemporary newspapers carry reports of fixtures being played in every wartime season. Unfortunately, there does not appear to be a club record of the wartime games played, but Skipton did issue fixture lists and have regular Annual General Meetings. Skipton probably had access to players from a number of neighbouring clubs that did not continue to play. The nearest club still playing in the final years of the war was Baildon. One of the handicaps that Skipton experienced was the distance it had to travel to play away fixtures. In the 1941/42 season Baildon, Harrogate Old Boys and Keighlians all featured in Skipton's fixture list. Baildon continued to feature in the Skipton fixture list in the later years of the war. Many of the players had to travel considerable distances to home games at Skipton's Sandylands ground. In the Skipton history it is recorded that one player's travelling schedule meant that he often arrived just before kick-off and so had to change in the train toilet as it neared Skipton. Skipton was very fortunate in that it had three members who are credited with keeping the club going during the war years. Bob Boothman, Rayner Garbutt and Dr James Robertson all had 'home' postings and were the men who organised fixtures and teams. Skipton's survival was in many ways similar to that of Pocklington and Selby – a club with enthusiastic officials and good links with local Services units.

Sheffield

In the south of the West Riding, Sheffield managed to continue to play fixtures at their Abbeydale Park ground for all of the wartime seasons. This was another remarkable achievement considering the extent of the bombing suffered by the city. Bombing raids on Sheffield began in August 1940 and continued until July 1942. The Sheffield Blitz on the 12th December 1940 was the most serious bombing raid and the bombs caused tremendous damage and loss of life across large parts of the city.

In the early part of the 1939/40 season, Sheffield Tigers, and the Sheffield based English Steel Corporation managed to play some games by combining their resources but both were struggling. In December 1939, in an attempt to resolve some of the problems caused by the lack of available players, a meeting was held in the Museum Hotel on Orchard Street. The purpose of the meeting was to form a Sheffield and District XV to enable rugby to continue in the city. The first fixture played by this team took place on Boxing Day 1939 when a Sheffield and District XV met a Glyn Davies Chesterfield XV. The proceeds from the game were donated to the Sheffield Newspapers War Relief Fund. The biggest game played by the District XV, in fact one of the biggest rugby union games ever to be played in the city, took place on 9th March 1940 at Sheffield United's Bramall Lane Ground. A Sheffield and District XV played against Derbyshire. An attendance of nearly 4,000 saw the Sheffield XV defeat Derbyshire by 28 points to 17 with funds raised at the match again going to the War Relief Fund. Sheffield contributed four players to the District team with others coming from a number of local clubs such as Sheffield Tigers, Doncaster, Rotherham and English Steel Corporation. Although Sheffield did not manage to play every Saturday during the wartime seasons, fixtures were arranged against Sheffield University, local schools, a number of Services teams and also Rotherham Home Guard. The club's Abbeydale Park Ground hosted regular rugby during the war although I do not think the club kept records of its wartime activities. The club historian, in his history of Sheffield RUFC, records the events in the 1939/40 season and suggests that from 1940 onwards there were occasional fixtures played involving a Sheffield and District team. Perhaps it was the Sheffield and District team that was playing through the war years. As there were no other clubs in action in this part of the West Riding, it is logical to assume that any locally based players who wanted a game would gravitate to Sheffield.

York

York began wartime rugby with the major handicap of no home ground. The club's pitch behind the Woodman Public House, in Bishopthorpe, a small village on the outskirts of the city, was requisitioned and ploughed up in order that crops could be grown. I believe that one of the main reasons that York survived, despite six seasons without a ground, was because of the efforts of the Secretary, Mr Ronnie Jackson. Having lost many playing members to the Yorkshire Hussars in 1939, Mr Jackson will have found it very difficult initially to find sufficient players for regular games but his enthusiasm and determination must have kept the club going. For the first two wartime seasons, both York and York Railway Institute were playing fixtures in the city. Both clubs organised games against Services XVs, St John's College and each other. In the 1940/41 season, York played against York Railway Institute on at least six occasions. 1940/41 was the last season that the Railway Institute played fixtures, but their ground on New Lane continued to be used by Services XVs and also by York. After York R.I. closed down, York's fixture list was made up of Services XVs, schools, St John's College, Selby and Pocklington. York was heavily bombed in April 1942 but that did not deter Ronnie Jackson who kept the club going through that difficult time. In the 1944/45 season, York announced a much more ambitious fixture list playing clubs such as Sale, Huddersfield Old Boys, Roundhay and Headingley Old Boys alongside their fixtures against the local Services units, school teams and Selby. Because of the lack of a home ground, York had a very nomadic existence during the war years. Home games were played at Archbishop Holgate School, St Peters School and New Lane. Anyone wishing to watch a York home game would have needed to check the Yorkshire Evening Press to confirm where it was taking place. York played some fixtures on York Rugby League Club's Clarence Street Ground. York Rugby League club had continued to play during the war and, the Royal Army Pay Corps XV was also based there. Any fixtures against the RAPC would therefore be played at Clarence Street. It was likely that on every Saturday of the season there would a rugby match taking place on the ground. Clarence

Street was also the venue for a charity match played on 22nd April, 1944, when York met a Cookes Athletic Club XV, with the proceeds being donated to the Red Cross York Prisoner Fund.

Harrogate Old Boys

I assume that Harrogate Old Boys the final club in the Survivors chapter did manage to play in every wartime season. However, because of a lack of records or evidence from local newspaper reports it is impossible to confirm this view. There are gaps when no reports of their activities exist, but this does not mean they were not playing fixtures.

Date	Opponents	Ground	Result	Score For	Score Against
1942					
September 19	Baildon	Home	Won	22	16
,, 26	R.A.F., Church Fenton	Home	Won	24	14
October 3	Old Leodiensians	Home	Won	16	8
,, 10	1st East Riding Yeomanry	Home	Won	9	8
,, 17	Baildon	Away	Scratched	—	—
,, 24	R.A.P.C.	Home	Won	6	3
,, 31	Leeds Home Guard	Home	Won	30	0
November 7	125th O.C.T.U., R.A.	Home	Draw	8	8
,, 14	9th F.T.R., R.A.	Home	Won	11	9
,, 21	Headingley Old Boys	Home			
,, 28	Leeds Medicals	Home			
December 5	1st East Riding Yeomanry	Home			
,, 12	Roundhay	Away			
,, 19	9th F.T.R., R.A.	Home			
,, 26	No. 7 P.R.C., R.A.F.	Home			
1943					
January 2	R. Signals	Home			
,, 9	R.A.F., York	Home			
,, 16	No. 7 P.R.C., R.A.F.	Home			
,, 23	R. Signals	Home			
,, 30	Roundhay	Home			
February 6	Leeds Home Guard	Away			
,, 13	R.A.F., York	Home			
,, 20	Headingley Old Boys	Away			
,, 27	R.A.P.C.	Away			
March 6	Leeds Medicals	Away			
,, 13	Hunslet Engineering Co.	Home			
,, 20	[illegible]	[illegible]			
,, 27	R.A.F., Church Fenton	Home			
April 3	125th O.C.T.U., R.A.	Home			
,, 10	Old Leodiensians	Away			
,, 17	Baildon	Away			

Harrogate Old Boys Fixtures for 1942-43

Sports coverage in the local and regional newspapers became very sparse in 1943 and early 1944 and even reports on the professional sports, soccer and rugby league, were often limited to a few lines once or twice a week. In my view, the fact that Harrogate Old Boys were playing fixtures at the beginning of the 1944/45 season strongly suggests that the club was a survivor.

There are records of Harrogate fixtures up to the end of the 1942/43 season and again in 1944/45.What happened in the 1943/44 season is not very clear. There are references to fixtures being played by the club in September 1943 and, as the club organised a fixture list for the first part of the 1944/45 season, I believe it safe to assume that the club must have been playing in the previous season. The other information that seems to support this view is the newspaper report of Harrogate's first fixture in the 1945/46 season against Roundhay. The captain for that fixture was C. Murray, who it was reported had captained the club two years earlier in 1943. One of the factors in Harrogate's survival must have been the large number of Services teams in the area. This meant that most of the wartime fixture lists were full of Army, RAF and on odd occasions Navy XVs. The Harrogate ground was also in regular use by Services XVs in order to entertain clubs like Roundhay and Headingley Old Boys.

Referees

An important factor in clubs continuing to play must have been the availability of referees. I imagine that all the clubs that survived will have had someone they could rely on to be at every home game. Wartime restrictions will have affected the ability of referees to travel far to referee games. Most clubs, as was the case at Huddersfield Old Boys, will have had the same referee for all their home games. Mr J. Wrigglesworth from Batley, refereed most of Huddersfield's games and he would have certainly been highly valued. However, I am sure that for some clubs, fixtures organised at short notice would have been refereed by one of the senior players or a retired member. Rugby union has always been a well disciplined sport and the respect for the referee shown by rugby players will have meant that games refereed by senior or retired players probably took place without incident.

Chapter Ten

The ones that nearly made it

There were a number of clubs that managed to continue to play after the 1939/40 season but did not continue through to the end of the war. For many of the clubs that re-started in September and October 1939, 1939/40 was the only season of wartime rugby that they played. The number of clubs that did manage to play during the 1939/40 season may have given the impression that Yorkshire rugby was continuing more or less as normal. The reality was very different once the 'Phoney Season' came to an end. As an increasing number of players were called up and rationing and travel restrictions really began to bite then for many clubs hard decisions had to be made. There were a number that did not play right through the war but did manage to play in 1940/41 and even one or two clubs that tried to re-start again in late 1940. The darkest days of the war and the impact of the hostilities on everyday life began to force many clubs to restrict their activities or close down.

Sadly, Halifax did not manage to continue playing despite the efforts made by its officials, in the early years of the war, to encourage other local clubs to play fixtures. In fact, it appears that by the middle of the war none of the Halifax District clubs were still in action. This must have been very disappointing for those officials who gave so much time and effort in 1939 and 1940 trying to keep the sport going. Did some Halifax based players gravitate to Huddersfield? It is a relatively short distance between the towns and this may explain why none of the Halifax clubs continued to play.

For some of the clubs that were still playing regularly across the County in 1942, the 1942/43 season was when they really began to struggle. I imagine that for some club officials the weekly problem of finding a team and opponents must have left them wondering whether it was better to close down and encourage any players still available to find an active club nearby.

For Old Leodiensians, who managed to play until the end of the 1942/43 season, there were opportunities for their players to play at Roundhay and Headingley Old Boys. Both were providing regular rugby and had full fixture lists that gave opportunities for Leeds based players to play regularly. Having managed to play fixtures for four difficult seasons it seems strange that Old Leodiensians should take the decision to stop organising fixtures. However, it could have simply been that the one or two people keeping the club going were either called up or were unable to carry on and there was no-one to take their place.

Keighlians played in the early years of the war, and then, like Old Leodiensians, closed down. However, like Old Leodiensians there were neighbouring clubs that continued. Skipton and Baildon were both within reasonable travelling distance and could have provided a game for any Keighlians players still able to play.

Sandal was successful in the early wartime seasons and played regular fixtures but then in 1941 decided not to continue allowing any players still available to join Wakefield Old Boys.

There were two clubs that did not re-start playing at the beginning of the war as neither of them was in existence in the 1930s. Hunslet Engine Company and Wakefield Old Boys both began playing regularly in the middle of the war and, as I mention in an earlier chapter, neither club continued to play after April 1945.

Hunslet Engine Company

Hunslet Engine Company began to play regular fixtures in the 1942/43 season, initially at Parkside, Hunslet Rugby League Club's ground, and then at Robin Hood after Old Leodiensians closed down. The team was organised by Mr Aubery Casewell, a Welsh Rugby League international who worked at the Engine Company as an engineers' fitter. Before the war Aubery Casewell had played for Salford and Leeds in a distinguished career in the professional code. In 1939 he signed for Hunslet Rugby League Club and played rugby league for Hunslet during the first two wartime seasons.

Aubery Casewell

The Hunslet Engine Company team he organised was very competitive and, as he was only thirty three when the team began playing fixtures, he may well have played the occasional game. Four of the Hunslet Engine Company's players, Freddie Williamson, Freddie Fletcher, Sam Sweeting and Don Burnell signed for Hunslet Rugby League Club and had successful careers in rugby league. As the Engine Company was in full production during the war, employing hundreds of local men, I am sure that Aubery Casewell did not have any difficulty finding fifteen players every Saturday in the rugby season. Aubery Casewell joined Featherstone Rovers Rugby League Club in 1944 as coach and after he left Featherstone he became heavily involved with the organisation of amateur rugby league in the Leeds area.

Wakefield Old Boys

I mentioned this club in an earlier chapter but I think it is worthy of further mention because of its similarity to what Eddie Waring, who later went on to have an illustrious career as a television commentator, did in rugby league at Dewsbury during the war. Eddie Waring had made Dewsbury one of the most successful wartime clubs. He attracted many internationals to the club's Crown Flatt ground where big crowds enjoyed watching some of the biggest rugby league names turning out in Dewsbury's colours. The Wakefield Old Boys organiser, Doug Lloyd, also attracted quality players, including internationals, to play in some of the club's fixtures. There were a number of Wakefield Old Boys players that turned professional and had successful careers with local rugby league clubs. Doug Lloyd also attracted some very interesting opponents for fixtures at Eastmoor, College Grove and even Belle Vue, the home of Wakefield Trinity Rugby League club. One of the games at Belle Vue took place on Easter Monday 1943 when a combined Wakefield Old Boys and Wakefield Trinity team beat a Northern Command Army XV by 19 points to 8. The Army XV included three rugby league internationals, Trevor Foster, the Bradford Northern second row forward being one of them. The fixture raised funds for the Clayton Hospital.

Welsh rugby union internationals, such as scrum half Price Stephens and stand- off Willie Jenkins who played his club rugby for Swansea, were amongst the big names that Doug Lloyd attracted to Wakefield. Jimmy Ledgard, a future rugby league international, was one of the Wakefield Old Boys who signed professional rugby league forms. Ledgard had played for Sandal prior to joining Wakefield Old Boys where he became one of their most prominent players. Another seven Wakefield Old Boy's players also turned professional, an indication of the strength of the club.

The success of Wakefield Old Boys must have helped Wakefield to make such a success of the first season of peacetime rugby. The Old Boys were playing regularly at College Grove, the Wakefield Ground, and when they closed down activities at the end of the 1944/45 season a number of their prominent local players must have returned to play for Wakefield in 1945/46.

The playing record of Wakefield Old Boys is very impressive over the four seasons it was in existence. The club played one hundred and twenty five games, won one hundred and six, lost fourteen and drew five. Given the quality of the opposition the Wakefield Old Boys played against this is even more remarkable. Doug Lloyd's ability to attract teams containing international and county players from both codes to Wakefield must have been helped by teams expecting the fixture to be highly competitive and knowing they would have to play very well to win. Unfortunately, Doug Lloyd's involvement in rugby after the war is not documented. He was obviously a very good organiser and it would be a surprise if his only involvement in rugby was with Wakefield Old Boys.

Chapter Eleven

The National Picture

The Rugby Football Union did not really operate as a National Governing Body during the war. The meetings that took place between 1939 and 1945 were usually held in London and only involved the London based committee members. At an early meeting it was agreed, by the London members, that for the duration of the war the Finance and Emergency Committee would act on behalf of the RFU. Obviously, it would have been difficult for the Governing Body of an amateur sport to get all the members of its committee to meet regularly. The members would have had to travel great distances to discuss issues that often affected parts of the country differently. Across England there were pockets of rugby activity that reflected the picture in Yorkshire but in reality there were also parts of the country where very little club rugby was played. National decisions may have had little relevance to local or regional rugby and would have been difficult to implement. Consequently, the announcements from the RFU between 1939 and 1945 were infrequent. However, the RFU Secretary, Mr S.F. Cooper, did write to all the County Unions in November 1939 as follows, *The Rugby Football Union Committee recommend that although the fixtures for the current season have been cancelled the county committees should encourage clubs to arrange fixtures with other clubs or Service XVs, and facilitate Service matches.'* The reality was that by November 1939, certainly in Yorkshire, many clubs were either back in action or considering organising fixtures. The other major announcement in the early years of the war concerned the involvement of rugby league players in wartime rugby union. After November 1939, the meetings of the Finance and Emergency Committee did continue to take place but it appears that no major issues were discussed.

The RFU was criticised for being inactive during the war. In its defence it cited the following reasons for this:

> Twickenham was out of the control of the RFU, having been requisitioned.
>
> Most of the players were in the forces.
>
> The activities of clubs had been curtailed in many parts of the country.
>
> The RFU committee members who were not in the forces were often unable to play an active role in managing rugby union at national level, mainly because of the difficulties and dangers involved in travelling to London.

One very positive move made by the RFU was when it successfully approached the Board of Trade for concessions for the supply of certificates to enable clubs to purchase footballs and additional clothing coupons to purchase jerseys. The Board of Trade did not want any publicity about this concession but County members of the RFU committee were informed so that they could pass this information on to the clubs that were still active.

Representative rugby at all levels was mainly organised by the Services. In 1940/41, the darkest days of the war, few representative fixtures took place. Food and transport difficulties and the rules on the assembly of large crowds were the main reasons for this. Once the rules on the size of crowds were relaxed and the tide turned in the war, more and more Services representative games took place.

The Service Internationals became a regular feature of the rugby union season, with big crowds and considerable sums of money raised for Services charities and the Red Cross.

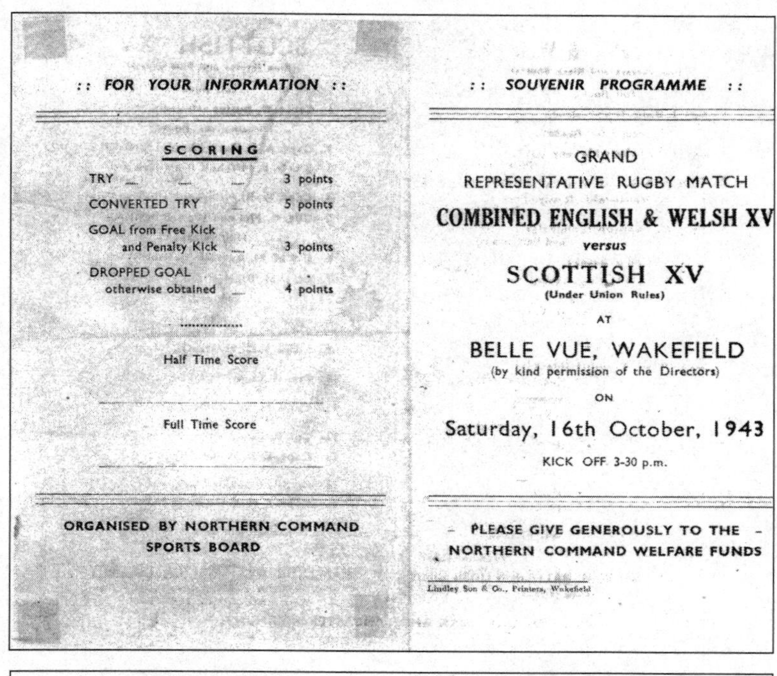

:: FOR YOUR INFORMATION ::

SCORING

TRY ... ... 3 points
CONVERTED TRY ... 5 points
GOAL from Free Kick and Penalty Kick ... 3 points
DROPPED GOAL otherwise obtained ... 4 points

Half Time Score

Full Time Score

ORGANISED BY NORTHERN COMMAND SPORTS BOARD

:: SOUVENIR PROGRAMME ::

GRAND
REPRESENTATIVE RUGBY MATCH

COMBINED ENGLISH & WELSH XV

versus

SCOTTISH XV

(Under Union Rules)

AT

BELLE VUE, WAKEFIELD

(by kind permission of the Directors)

ON

Saturday, 16th October, 1943

KICK OFF 3-30 p.m.

– PLEASE GIVE GENEROUSLY TO THE –
NORTHERN COMMAND WELFARE FUNDS

Lindley Son & Co., Printers, Wakefield

Combined English & Welsh XV

(White Jerseys and Black Shorts)

Full Back:

1—Cpl. J. Bond (Cumberland)

Threequarter Backs:

2—Lt. H. L. Talbot-Harvey (Oxford University)
3—Capt. J. A. S. Taylor (Leicestershire)
4—Lt. J. H. Reichwald (Rosslyn Park & Surrey)
5—Lt. J. C. Swanson (Cambridge U. and Barbarians)

Half Backs:

6—Lt. P. R. H. Hastings (Welsh Guards & England)
7—Capt. J. Ellis (Wakefield, Yorkshire & England)

Forwards:

8—Gdsmn. C. Williams (Llanelly)
9—Capt. J. S. Stones (Oxford University)
10—Cdt. Hogg (Oxford University)
11—Maj. T. A. Hall (London Serves & Army)
12—Lt. B. J. A. Love (London Welsh, Middlesex)
13—Cdt. C. H. Sture (Devon County)
14—Bdr. J. Reeve (Leicestershire)
15—Gdsmn. S. Davies (Welsh Guards, Swansea)

SCOTTISH XV

(Blue Jerseys and Blue Shorts)

Full Back:

1—Sergt. G. Butler (Hawick)

Threequarter Backs:

2—Capt. A. L. Barr (West of Scotland)
3—S/I. D. F. Mitchell (Galashiels and West of Scotland)
4—Capt. D. R. McGregor (Rosslyn Park)
5—Cdt. C. McLean (East of Scotland)

Half Backs:

6—C.S.M. M. Burrell (Galashiels)
7—Lt. J. M. Blair (Oxford U. & Scotland)

Forwards:

8—Sgmn. L. W. Adkin (Edinburgh Wanderers)
9—L/Cpl. J. D. H. Hastie (Melrose & Scotland)
10—Pte. G. Lees (Galashiels and Scottish Trials)
11—Capt. N. W. Ramsey (Army and Scotland)
12—Cpl. R. Cowe (Melrose & Scotland)
13—Capt. E. E. Wilson (Queens U., Belfast)
14—Pte. A. Crawford (Melrose)
15—Capt. J. N. Gadzow (Edinburgh Wanderers)

Referee: Mr. GORDON WHITTAKER. Touch Judges: Capt. H. COUPE and Capt. H. N. PRICE.

HALF TIME TUG-OF-WAR

SECOND ARMOURED BATTALION (Irish Guards) v SHARLSTON WEST WALTON COLLIERY

GREEN JERSEYS

(NORTHERN COUNTY CHAMPIONS)
RED AND WHITE JERSEYS

BAND OF THE YORK AND LANCASTER REGIMENT.

A wartime representative fixture

Could the RFU have been more active during wartime? I doubt that it could. Where the sport did continue to take place, it was often because of local enthusiasts who did not really need involvement from the Governing Body in order for them to continue. The majority of issues the clubs faced during the war were local and often involved travel, the availability of grounds, players, fixtures, and the impact of the bombing on their area. All of these issues were better resolved locally and it is difficult to see what a more active RFU could have done in the circumstances.

Chapter Twelve

The relationship with Rugby League

Following the outbreak of war the Rugby Football League responded very differently to the Rugby Football Union. Perhaps it was because rugby league was played mainly in a relatively small geographical area in the North of England and it was also a professional sport with financial commitments. Were these the reasons that the sport was able to react quickly to the declaration of war? Or had senior RFL officials made contingency plans? Whatever the reason, Emergency Leagues were quickly established and fixtures for most clubs began on the 16th September 1939.

As the 1939/40 season got into full swing, the issue of rugby league players playing rugby union became more of a problem for the RFU than it was for the RFL. The selection in October 1939 by Roundhay of Jim Brough, the former Leeds Rugby League player, had obviously brought the issue of rugby league players taking part in rugby union to the attention of the authorities. I think that most people involved in club rugby union believed that the outbreak of war would see the suspension of the professionalism rules and that clubs would be free to select whoever the wished. Perhaps that would have been the case if the selection of Jim Brough by Roundhay had not been highlighted in the press. Whether it was the publicity around Jim Brough's selection, or the possibility of rugby league players being selected by Services teams, is unclear. Whatever the reason, proposals regarding rugby league players were made by the RFU committee on 13th October 1939. If the proposals were approved, they would cover all the possible situations where a rugby league player in the Services could be selected to take part in a rugby union game. The initial proposals from the RFU included allowing a rugby union club to include a rugby league player belonging to His Majesty's Forces in a fixture against another rugby union club. This particular item appeared to be the most controversial and, when the proposals were voted on as a whole, a tie resulted. A postal vote was then held regarding the proposal that rugby league players should be allowed to take part in club versus club fixtures. The postal vote resulted in that particular proposal being defeated by twenty four votes to seventeen. A new resolution without the contentious club versus club proposal was therefore put forward as follows:

1. A rugby union XV may play against a Services team containing players who have played rugby league.

2. A rugby union XV may include rugby league players belonging to the forces when playing Services teams.

3. The Emergency resolutions are for the period of the war and apply to rugby league players who have had no connection with rugby league since their enlistment.

The new proposals were agreed and rugby union clubs were informed about the rules on rugby league players in a statement released to the press on 13th November 1939. When he was informed, John Wilson, the Secretary of the Rugby Football League, welcomed the decision and said, *'I am very glad. It is a proper thing that all men in the Army should be allowed to play football together without any restrictions.*

During the last war there were no conditions and already in this war matches between Services teams have included rugby league players. Now, however rugby league men can now take part in games against civilian clubs.'

Apart from John Wilson's positive response to the RFU decision, there was very little public reaction from the rugby league clubs or the RFL itself. The issue of rugby league players being included in Army rugby union teams was raised at an RFL Emergency Committee meeting on 5th March 1940 but consideration of the issue was deferred for six months. I cannot find any reference to the matter being discussed again, so I can only assume that the RFL did not consider it a cause for concern.

Did rugby league players take part in club versus club games? I think almost certainly in Yorkshire they did. Pocklington was a club that welcomed the involvement of players from both codes; I hardly think they were alone. Many wartime fixtures were not reported and team lists were not submitted to a Governing Body. I am therefore sure that if a man appeared at a rugby union ground with a pair of boots and a request to play, he would be welcomed especially in the dark days of the war when the clubs that were playing often struggled to find fifteen players. Another reason for my belief was that certainly in York, and probably in other rugby league towns, rugby union players were playing for professional rugby league clubs with no obvious sanctions being imposed on them. In York the professional rugby league club was quite open about including rugby union players in its team. On 13th March 1943, W.E. Jones, a Welsh international who had played his club rugby for Swansea and Neath, was included in the York team that played at Leeds in the Rugby League Challenge Cup. York lost the game but Jones made a good impression. The rugby league club was keen to include him the following week but he was required to be in Wales for a club fixture. Around this time, York were including a number of other rugby union players in their teams, reporting that fact in the local newspapers. Evidently neither they nor the players received any sanctions. There were many international rugby union players stationed in the North of England and it is very unlikely that it was only W.E. Jones who played for a professional rugby league club.

The dispensation that the RFU granted for rugby league players in the Services lasted until the end of the 1945/46 season.

During the war years the impact of rugby league players on the outcome of representative fixtures was often very significant. In fact, at a RFL Emergency Committee meeting held in 1943, the members were recorded as being delighted with the performance of rugby league players in a Services International. Once hostilities ended, there were clubs and some RFU officials who wanted the strict rules regarding rugby league players re-imposing. A proposal by the Manchester club was put to the RFU Annual General Meeting on 22nd June 1945 that the concessions given to rugby league players should be removed immediately. The proposal was discussed at an RFU Committee meeting on 7th September, 1945 when it was agreed that rugby league players could continue to play rugby union for Services teams during the 1945/46 season. As a result, a number of the representative fixtures played during the season had rugby league players taking part.

In Yorkshire there was a good relationship between John Wilson, the RFL Secretary, and Bob Oakes, the Yorkshire RFU Secretary. Both men corresponded regularly and often met at important games. Bob Oakes, as mentioned in an earlier chapter, supported the dispensation that the RFU had given to rugby league players. Mr Oakes had, in fact, approached the RFU regarding the issue of Jim Brough being selected for Roundhay, suggesting that the 'free gangway' that applied in World War One should apply. John Wilson was invited onto the Northern Command Sports Board and in that role was very supportive of the many rugby league players that took part in the Northern Command

PROCEEDS TO THE A.P.T.C. BENEVOLENT FUND

Please Give Generously !

	AN ARMY XV. (Red)		A.P.T.C. XV. (PAST AND PRESENT) (Black and White)	
		Full Back		
15	Cpl. E. Ward, Bradford Northern and England		C.S.M.I. F. Trott, Penarth, Army, and Wales	15
		Threequarters		
14	Mjr. T. G. H. Jackson, Army		S.I. R. L. Francis, Barrow and England	14
13	Capt. J. R. Henderson, London Scottish		S.I. J. A. Gregory, Aldershot Services and Army	13
12	Lt. L. G. Gloag, Services International		S.I. D. Y. Morley, Halifax R.L.	12
11	Lt. I. John—Aberavon		S.I. W. Dockar—Hull R.L.	11
		Half-Backs		
10	Capt. B. P. Hepburn, Woodford		Capt. A. J. Risman, Salford, Army, and Wales	10
9	Lt. W. J. L. Ellis, Bath, Bristol and Yorkshire		C.S.M.I. J. Radcliffe	9
		Forwards		
8	Cdt. P. C. G. Ballingall, Aldershot Services		Capt. A. A. Brown, Exeter, Devon, and England	8
7	Pte. F. Hill—Bristol		S.I. C. Ambrose, London District	7
6	Cdt. F. G. Horsell, Aldershot Services		S.I. D. Prosser, Leeds R. L. and Wales	6
5	Capt. L. M. Burcher, Aldershot Services		C.S.M.I. W. G. Swift, Cumberland	5
4	Tpr. Hooper—R.A.C.		S.I. Jones—London District	4
3	Pte. D. F. White, Northampton and Army		S.I. J. Priest—Bristol	3
2	Lt. R. A. Brown, Richmond and Army		S.I. G. S. Brown, Batley R. L. and England	2
1	Sgt. T. G. P. Rodgers, Aldershot Services		S.I. E. Tattersfield, Batley R. L. and England	1

Referee - GORDON WHITTAKER

Touch Judges

S.Q.M.S. J. YARKER, R.A.P.C., and L/Cpl. B. MARLOW, R. Sigs.

THE BAND OF THE

WEST YORKSHIRE REGIMENT

A representative fixture played in 1946

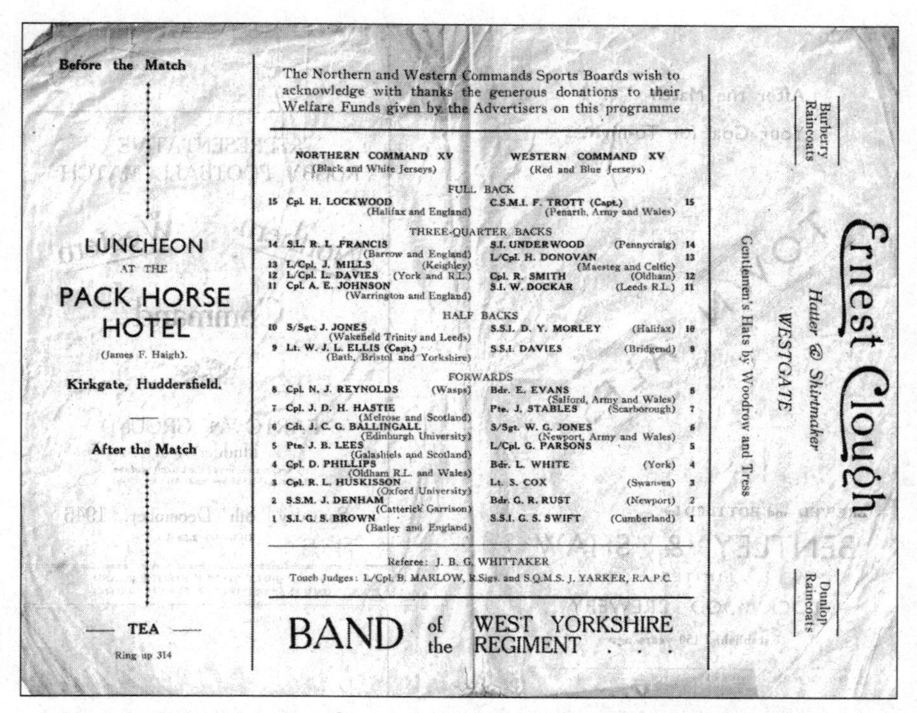
Before the Match

LUNCHEON
AT THE
PACK HORSE HOTEL
(James F. Haigh).
Kirkgate, Huddersfield.

After the Match

— TEA —
Ring up 314

The Northern and Western Commands Sports Boards wish to acknowledge with thanks the generous donations to their Welfare Funds given by the Advertisers on this programme

No.	NORTHERN COMMAND XV (Black and White Jerseys)	WESTERN COMMAND XV (Red and Blue Jerseys)	No.
	FULL BACK		
15	Cpl. H. LOCKWOOD (Halifax and England)	C.S.M.I. F. TROTT (Capt.) (Penarth, Army and Wales)	15
	THREE-QUARTER BACKS		
14	S.I. R. L. FRANCIS (Barrow and England)	S.I. UNDERWOOD (Pennycraig)	14
13	L/Cpl. J. MILLS (Keighley)	L/Cpl. H. DONOVAN (Maesteg and Celtic)	13
12	L/Cpl. L. DAVIES (York and R.L.)	Cpl. R. SMITH (Oldham)	12
11	Cpl. A. E. JOHNSON (Warrington and England)	S.I. W. DOCKAR (Leeds R.L.)	11
	HALF BACKS		
10	S/Sgt. J. JONES (Wakefield Trinity and Leeds)	S.S.I. D. Y. MORLEY (Halifax)	10
9	Lt. W. J. L. ELLIS (Capt.) (Bath, Bristol and Yorkshire)	S.S.I. DAVIES (Bridgend)	9
	FORWARDS		
8	Cpl. N. J. REYNOLDS (Wasps)	Bdr. E. EVANS (Salford, Army and Wales)	8
7	Cpl. J. D. H. HASTIE (Melrose and Scotland)	Pte. J. STABLES (Scarborough)	7
6	Cdt. J. C. G. BALLINGALL (Edinburgh University)	S/Sgt. W. G. JONES (Newport, Army and Wales)	6
5	Pte. J. B. LEES (Galashiels and Scotland)	L/Cpl. G. PARSONS	5
4	Cpl. D. PHILLIPS (Oldham R.L. and Wales)	Bdr. L. WHITE (York)	4
3	Cpl. R. L. HUSKISSON (Oxford University)	Lt. S. COX (Swansea)	3
2	S.S.M. J. DENHAM (Catterick Garrison)	Bdr. G. R. RUST (Newport)	2
1	S.I. G. S. BROWN (Batley and England)	S.S.I. G. S. SWIFT (Cumberland)	1

Referee: J. B. G. WHITTAKER

Touch Judges: L/Cpl. B. MARLOW, R.Sigs. and S.Q.M.S. J. YARKER, R.A.P.C.

BAND of the WEST YORKSHIRE REGIMENT . . .

Burberry Raincoats

Ernest Clough
Hatter & Shirtmaker
WESTGATE
Gentlemen's Hats by Woodrow and Tress

Dunlop Raincoats

A Services Representative fixture – both teams include rugby league players

fixtures. As well as being very positive about John Wilson's involvement with the Northern Command, the RFL was also very responsive to any rugby union requests for help. They supported the rugby union versus rugby league fixtures and were always happy to approve rugby union fixtures played on rugby league grounds.

Between 1939 and 1945 the majority of rugby league grounds in Yorkshire staged rugby union fixtures. On 14th October 1939 Fartown, the home of Huddersfield Rugby League Club, was used for a challenge match played under rugby union rules between a Huddersfield XV and team from men from the Anti -Aircraft Battery. The Huddersfield team contained a number of high profile rugby league players. Many Yorkshire rugby league grounds were used by local Services units for their home games. The representative fixtures that increased in number as the war progressed were mainly played on rugby league grounds. The relationship between rugby league and rugby union in Yorkshire was very positive right through the war. Clubs and officials from both codes were always prepared to support each other. They worked together to encourage men, particularly those in the Services, to continue to play sport as means of keeping up morale. They also contributed time and effort to the many fund raising fixtures that took place between 1939 and 1945.

The 'status quo' returned in 1946 when the RFU re-imposed its strict rules regarding rugby league players. It would be nearly fifty years before rugby union became a professional sport and all the barriers between the codes were lifted. Would rugby union be different today if the enlightened attitude to rugby league that prevailed during the war had continued? We will never know, but it is interesting to speculate on which code would have benefitted most.

Chapter Thirteen

Conclusion

Before I conclude this story, I thought it was important to include the only contemporary account I have found of Yorkshire rugby union in World War Two. Written by the then Yorkshire Secretary, Bob Oakes, it appeared in the 1946/47 Yorkshire Handbook as follows:

THE WAR YEARS

Season 1939-40 to Season 1945-46

By R.F. Oakes Honorary Secretary Y. R. F. U.

All was set to begin, on the 1st September 1939, another glorious season of Rugger. How keenly every Rugger player was looking forward to it. But, alas! The war trumpet sounded, and that month, for the second time in the memory of every Rugger man's life, saw the immediate closing down of the game, for the much more serious, and embittered game – WAR.

With a common understanding, and in no uncertain manner, the clubs of the four Home Unions, and in all our Dominions, put up the shutters on Rugger, forgetting, in the face of the vastness of a World War, that such a thing as Rugger ever existed. The ghastly tragedy of it all! How would it all end? Not that there was ever in the minds of anybody of the final result. So the Rugger man, along with his contemporaries of other branches of British sport, settled down to the serious side of things in the Army, the Royal Navy, the Air

Force, the Civil Defence, and the N. F. S. And so on – anything he was commanded to join and no matter where. Club, County and International Rugger had only a poor second place in the minds of these men. And so it remained until victory was assured, and the great upheaval of all that was considered finest and best on this earth, had come to an end and hostilities ceased in August 1945. Amidst the tragedy of it all, Rugger, although badly bent, was never actually broken, and several of the clubs in Britain managed, goodness only knows how, to stage a fair number of games, made possible by the old greybeards turning out supported by youths too young to then enlist, and Servicemen either home on leave or stationed somewhere near a Rugger centre.

But the vast majority of the clubs were compelled to close down, lock stock and barrel, for the duration. There were no regrets, for a thing had to be done – and done it was. The dire menace of those six awful war years is over, leaving death and destruction in its horrible trail certainly, but producing in the breasts of all a deep and sincere feeling of gratefulness and thankfulness that this old world still revolves on its axis.

Yet – there is still one hallowed regret, and one that is indelibly inscribed on the tablets of all our memories – those magnificent men who have played their last great game and given their all, and who are to-day sleeping peacefully all over the face of the globe. 'In some corner of a foreign field, that is forever England'. They will never be forgotten. God forbid that it should ever be otherwise, for these men gave quiet inspiration to the weak and distressed and a guiding hand to the uncertain, yes, in all walks of life.

'There's none of these so lonely and poor of old. But, dying has left us rarer gifts than gold.'

Despite all the ravages of war, this great game of ours refused to die, although terribly mauled and wounded. The various 'Commands' in the Army; the Northern Command, the Southern Command, the

Western Command and the Scottish Command, together with the Commands of the Air Force, and the Royal Navy (when they had an opportunity) came strongly into evidence and developed remarkably fine sides which included a number of well-known Rugby League players serving in H. M. Forces, the Rugby Football Union having already decreed that their law on professionalism should be eased 'for the duration', on the principle 'that if a man was good enough to fight with, he was equally good enough to play with' – a right and proper view without a doubt.

'Command' matches were organised all over the four Home Unions and games were played in England, Scotland, Wales and Ireland, many being games of an international character.

The termination of hostilities in August 1945 saw a brave attempt to resuscitate the game more fully, and activities were commenced in each of the four countries, not only by the clubs themselves, but by the various County Unions, and the Rugby Unions of England, Scotland, Wales and Ireland.

County games were re-established for season 1945/46, although it was agreed to ignore the County Championship Rule in regard to County qualification for that particular season only, so that any player not actually qualified by birth or residence could play for the County in which he happened to be at that time stationed.

Representative international games were also arranged between the four Home Unions, although no cap was allotted. Counties also followed this lead, and these County games did not carry any qualification for a county cap.

During the season a tremendous fillip was given to the game by the formation, from Servicemen in the New Zealand Army and Air Force, of three remarkably fine Rugger sides, one, the 'Kiwis' as they came to be known, the finest of the three, rising almost to the great heights of the famous 'All Blacks' of 1905-06 season, beating England, Ireland

and Wales, and only succumbing to the fine side Scotland put out at Murrayfield and also against Monmouthshire.

So, season 1945-46 saw the re-start of the game proper in Britain. Although play was not actually up to pre-war standard, it was clear to any observer that the old time keenness was still manifest, and today, all clubs, Counties and Countries are looking keenly forward to next season, and if perchance there is still hard spadework in plenty before all, it is felt that the game will quickly recover its old-time glory.'

Although the Yorkshire RFU was largely inactive during the war, Bob Oakes certainly was not. He organised representative fixtures and was also heavily involved in ensuring that the annual Christmas holiday schoolboy games that often took place at Headingley's Kirkstall Ground still went ahead.

Bob Oakes, in his account of wartime rugby activity, does not give any details of the games that were played but he does paint an interesting picture of how the sport reacted. As he points out in his article, rugby union in the County was certainly bent but not broken. The clubs that continued to play provided an opportunity for some normality in what, for many people, was the most difficult period of their lives. Without the efforts of the small band of enthusiasts at the clubs that continued, those opportunities could not have been provided. Unfortunately, because very few records exist today, it has been possible to name only a few of those enthusiasts. It was in most cases just one or two people at each club that managed to keep rugby alive and sadly, at some clubs, their efforts were not recognised or recorded. I hope that mentioning a few of these people here will mean that at least some record will exist of their contribution and bring that of others to mind.

At the end of this book I mention some of the Yorkshire rugby players who died for their country in World War Two. I am sure the list is not complete and that there were others who died in the war who had connections with Yorkshire rugby. I hope that some of the people whose names I do not know have been recognised by their clubs in previous times.

I have enjoyed this opportunity to delve into a largely unexplored period in rugby union history. Apart from at Huddersfield and Baildon much of what happened between 1939 and 1945 is missing from club records and in some cases, club histories. This is a pity, as keeping rugby going during the war was probably a much more difficult task than any subsequently encountered by the sport's administrators. Will some rugby enthusiasts who read this story be surprised to hear that their club played during the Second World War? I am sure some will, as over the months spent researching this story I have uncovered facts that have surprised one or two club historians whose records halted in 1939 and re-started in 1945.

If your club was active in World War Two and does not feature in this book, I apologise. I have attempted to reflect what happened through contemporary newspaper reports and the few records that do exist. As with all books of this type, as soon as they go to print new information emerges, and if that is the case with *Let Them Play By All Means,* please do not hesitate to contact me and share what you know.

I hope that you have enjoyed reading this story of a time that I think is best summed up by a phrase used in an earlier chapter, that Yorkshire rugby union in World War Two was '*a matter of improvisation.*'

Well done to all who carried this through.

References

Sheffield RUFC – The History by Andrew Reichwald

Pocklington at War by Jim and Margaret Ainsworth

History of the Rugby Football Union by O.L. Owen

A Social History of English Rugby Union by Tony Collins

Rugby League in War Time by John Schleppi